Tangible Equity

Move beyond the "why" of equity and learn what it actually looks like in the classroom. This powerful book by bestselling author Colin Seale shows how you can overcome barriers and create sustainable pathways to realizing equity for your students.

Part I of the book explains why all education stakeholders should not just prioritize equity, but go beyond the buzzwords. Part II looks at why good intentions aren't enough, and provides six ways you can leverage your power to really start doing something about equity. Part III discusses the five classroom-level philosophical shifts needed to make real change, including how to think differently about gifted education and achievement gaps. Finally, Part IV offers a variety of practical strategies for making equity real in your classrooms, no matter what grade level or subject area you teach. Throughout each chapter, you'll find stories, examples, and research to bring the ideas to life.

With the concrete suggestions in this book, you'll be able to overcome deficit models, focus on opportunities for academic success and educational justice, and make equity tangible for each of your students.

Colin Seale is an educator, attorney, and critical thinking expert. He founded thinkLaw, an award-winning organization, to help educators leverage inquiry-based instructional strategies that can close the critical thinking gap and ensure they teach and reach all students.

Tangible Equity

A Guide for Leveraging Student Identity, Culture, and Power to Unlock Excellence In and Beyond the Classroom

Colin Seale

NEW YORK AND LONDON

Cover image: © Getty Images

First published 2022
by Routledge
605 Third Avenue, New York, NY 10158

and by Routledge
4 Park Square, Milton Park, Abingdon, Oxon, OX14 4RN

Routledge is an imprint of the Taylor & Francis Group, an informa business

Library of Congress Cataloging-in-Publication Data
A catalog record for this title has been requested

ISBN: 978-1-032-25278-0 (hbk)
ISBN: 978-1-032-16178-5 (pbk)
ISBN: 978-1-003-28246-4 (ebk)

DOI: 10.4324/9781003282464

Typeset in Palatino
by SPi Technologies India Pvt Ltd (Straive)

Printed in the United Kingdom
by Henry Ling Limited

I dedicate this book to the people who made me think, made me love, made me feel, and made me, period. This work would be impossible without the sacrifices, unshakeable belief, inspiration, and joyful love I've gained from Granny Morris, Granny Seale, my mother Ruth and my amazing aunts and uncles, my siblings Roslyn, Roxanne and Colin III, my very special children Rose and Oliver and their amazing mom Carrie, and the countless friends, family members, and colleagues who constantly push me to fight for a better world and a better me.

Contents

Figures

Meet the Author

Colin Seale was born and raised in Brooklyn, NY, where struggles in his upbringing gave birth to his passion for educational equity. Tracked early into gifted and talented programs, Colin was afforded opportunities his neighborhood peers were not. Using lessons from his experience as a math teacher, later as an attorney, and now as a keynote speaker, contributor to Forbes, The 74, Edutopia and Education Post and author of Thinking Like a Lawyer: A Framework for Teaching Critical Thinking to All Students (Prufrock Press, 2020), Colin founded thinkLaw (www.thinklaw.us), a multi-award-winning organization to help educators leverage inquiry-based instructional strategies to close the critical thinking gap and ensure they teach and reach all students, regardless of race, zip code, or what side of the poverty line they are born into. In 2021, Colin launched The BEE Project, a non-profit organization redefining who qualifies as gifted and who gets to teach gifted children by inspiring, training, and certifying Black and Latinx educators to equitably design and lead gifted programs. These programs identify and meet the unique needs of brilliant Black and Latinx children and their families who have been overlooked and underestimated by our current system. When he's not serving as the world's most fervent critical thinking advocate or tweeting from @ColinESeale, Colin proudly serves as the world's greatest entertainer to his two young children.

Part I

The "Why" of Tangible Equity

Introduction

Equity for What?

Educational equity is not that complicated, right? We can visualize the common equality vs. equity graphic with the three boys watching a baseball game behind the fence where they all get one crate to stand on. And with that one crate, only one boy is tall enough to see over the fence. The other two are out of luck. But in the adjacent picture, the shorter boy gets two crates and the even shorter boy gets three crates. Just like that, all three can see over the fence. This is supposed to explain the difference between equity and equality, reasoning that equally distributing the crates does not do enough to create access and opportunity for all children. Of course, it is not really that simple.

To be fair, there is an obvious benefit from understanding that equity requires, at a minimum, an appreciation that student success at an individual level means not all students receive the same type or same amount of support to get there. But what if equity required more than differentiated supports? What happens when we probe deeper and ask "equity for what?" In this case, equity means that all three children will now have access to watch a baseball game from outside the fence, watching a roaring crowd of fans enjoy the game from inside the stadium. That does not seem like an equitable result, but it reminds me so much of the lackluster equity outcomes many educators advocate for in our school systems today.

DOI: 10.4324/9781003282464-2

Growing up in Brooklyn, New York, I experienced the "equity for what" disconnect in a very troubling way. As a child of immigrants growing up on free and reduced lunch in a single parent home with an incarcerated father, I was the prototype of the child who needed more crates than normal. A strike of good fortune led to my school identifying me as gifted and talented despite (or more likely, because of) my frequent behavior challenges and speech impediments. There was no gifted program in my Crown Heights neighborhood, so I received a crate in the form of transportation to a school in a different neighborhood.

When it was time for high school, my family acted like I won the lottery when I passed the exam to attend the Bronx High School of Science, one of New York City's specialized high schools that admitted very few Black and Latinx students then (and even fewer today[1]). What did I win in this lottery? Lots of crates! Now, I had access to a school that was incredibly successful at helping mostly Asian and white students who were already academically successful continue to be successful. I was no longer on a twenty-minute ride on the school bus like in elementary school. Now, I commuted ninety minutes each way because all three high schools within a short walk or bus ride were dropout factories at the time.

Again, I ask, equity for what? My mother immigrated to the United States from Barbados in the 1970s as one of seven children who were all well-versed in this unfair, but truthful message: "you're going to have to work twice as hard to get half as far." She raised me to understand that as a Black boy growing up in the struggle, I similarly needed to "work twice as hard to get half as far." I can feel the head nods and hear the "umm-hmms" of educators I partner with across the country who were similarly raised with this messaging. Since launching thinkLaw, an organization I founded to help educators and families close the critical gap by applying "Thinking Like a Lawyer" approaches to teaching and parenting, I am embarrassed to admit that thousands of educators across the country admit growing up under "work twice as hard to get half as far" rules. I see this unfair burden and I ask again, equity for what?

I think often about my blessed and highly favored K-12 journey. First, there was my accidental gifted education identification. Then, I dealt with all sorts of academic and life challenges in high school, graduating with my computer science degree from Syracuse University, serving as a gap-closing educator in Washington, DC and Las Vegas, Nevada, finishing law school at the top of my class while teaching during the day, practicing at a world-class law firm. And now, I built this innovative, award-winning organization thinkLaw that transformed my obsession with critical thinking into a powerful set of curricular resources and professional learning for school systems impacting millions of students across the country. And for all this, my story is often deemed "an exception to the rule." This rule normalizes, and often celebrates the inherently inequitable idea of watching the baseball game from outside of the fence. The question remains, equity for what?

I cannot raise my daughter and son to simply work twice as hard to half as far when I know a truly equitable system should not require some to exert extraordinary effort to obtain ordinary results. I cannot call it equity when a few more Black and Brown students in New York City have access to a school requiring a three-hour, round-trip commute while other students in New York City can walk to an excellent high school in their own neighborhood. I cannot continue to celebrate social media posts with the hashtag #BlackGirlMagic, despite the joy I feel when these posts show brilliant Black women earning their doctorate degrees, enrolling in prestigious medical residency programs, or doing the wide variety of amazing outcomes brilliant Black women are and have always been capable of. I am angry at the reality that for so many brilliant Black girls who are out here working twice as hard to get half as far, it *still* requires #BlackGirlMagic for them to achieve excellent outcomes in life.

Give me 100 crates to stand on, but if I am still watching the game from outside of the fence, that's not equity. If I'm still celebrating stories like mine as exceptions to the rule instead of attacking the still-too-predictable rule that where you are born and who you are born to will determine your outcomes in life, that's not equity, either. Equity means #BlackGirlMagic is no longer required for brilliant Black girls to obtain excellent outcomes. Equity means we are building a new system where all students have a true shot at being exceptional. Equity means we recognize that this is not just hard work, this is heart work.

In this book, I define equity without crates, without a fence, and without any preconceived notion that my students even want to watch a baseball game. Equity is about reducing the predictive power of demographics and zip codes to determine the success of young people inside and outside of the classroom to zero. Equity would mean I would not be able to see a child from rural Arkansas who is the third generation of her family in a trailer park where most families are economically disadvantaged and have great odds in guessing that she and other children in her community are not succeeding academically. Equity would mean there would be no more news stories when the child of undocumented parents in a border community gets full-ride scholarships to all the Ivy League universities. This is the equity of my hopes and my dreams.

The Tangible Equity difference is that this book is not just about these pie-in-the-sky outcomes we can simply wish for as part of our collective hopes and dreams. This is about the practical, Tuesday-morning-in-October instructional strategies educators, leaders, and families can use to give our children explicit permission to dare, to dream, to question, and to build the equitable system we have long deserved. Tangible Equity is about understanding that who our students are, how they are, where they are, and why they are can and must be leveraged to accelerate their learning outcomes. Tangible Equity is about the adults in the room naming their explicit biases, fears, and doubts about their ability to make change at a systemic level and recognizing that this is not and was never about them.

The history of the world is a history of young people changing the world, so the Tangible Equity approaches described in this book will help you hold up a mirror to children to help them see and understand their power, embrace and nurture this power, and help them apply their power to "be the change." Through concrete instructional strategies and tools, you will help our young people excel academically and navigate the system we currently have while also helping them use their knowledge and power to build the system *they* believe we deserve.

If you are looking for a text that teaches students what to think, this is wrong book. This is about young people learning *how* to think. If you are seeking a guide to navigate how to embed Critical Race Theory (CRT) in schools or make your school system more anti-racist, this is also the wrong book. I refuse to entertain the questionable debate of CRT being taught in schools because I am certain the CRT conversation would not exist if we cared more about RCT: raising critical thinkers.

In the work I've led across the United States in rural, urban, suburban, affluent, and high-poverty school systems with a broad range of demographics and political leanings, I have never met an educator or parent who disagrees with the idea that children should learn how to think critically. I have never met an educator or parent who disagrees with the idea that the quintessential, "anyone can make it" view of The American Dream ought to be a reality for all regardless of the circumstances they are born into. This is not some sort of fringe, uber-progressive, super "woke" ideology; Tangible Equity applies regardless of the dominant political or religious beliefs of your community, their views on whether, how, and to what extent schools should discuss current events and potentially controversial issues in schools, and the racial demographics of your school system's teaching and student populations.

This book is for anyone who is serious about the beyond-the-crates view of equity that reduces the power of demographic predictability. This book is for anyone who already understands why educational equity is necessary and what equity may look like in theory, but lacks practical guidance on what it takes to make educational equity actionable at the district, school, classroom, and individual student levels. This book is for school systems who care deeply about this work, who have written bold equity-related resolutions, grounded their strategic plans in equity, but still struggle with high levels of demographic predictability in their academic and disciplinary inequities despite this boldness. This book is for classroom teachers who have read all the books, gone to all the workshops, and had lots of courageous conversations about race but feel very uncourageous knowing that all their good intentions and deep belief in the importance of equity has not translated into meaningful change for their students in and beyond their classrooms.

Part I of this book will explain why all education stakeholders should prioritize the beyond-the-buzzwords framework of Tangible Equity. This section of the book also makes the historical, ethical, and practical case for creating an educational system that views the diverse identities and strengths of our students as *the* pathway for an asset-based, identity-affirming, and transformational model for academic excellence.

Tangible Equity is biased towards action. Part II of this book outlines the "how" of these actions by breaking down why good intentions are not enough. Going much deeper, this section gives all stakeholders in education a concrete "how" on leveraging your power to identify and successfully achieve and sustain crucial equity priorities.

In Part III, this book discusses the classroom-level philosophical shifts that must occur to make equity real at the classroom level. This section argues vehemently for a systemic approach to prioritizing excellence through gifted education, advanced academics and nurturing brilliance. Instead of speaking in platitudes about what schools should do for "all" children to close achievement gaps, Part III of Tangible Equity will shift your thinking toward to a more personalized equitable lens – shifting form "all" students to "each" child - with an eye towards moving beyond closing achievement gaps so we can start talking about what it takes to shatter achievement ceilings.

In Part IV, this book breaks down the identity-driven excellence model that has guided the work I have used to help school systems design curriculum-agnostic frameworks that make equity real at the classroom level in all grade levels and subject areas. This is a "because, not despite" model that will give readers the tools they need to see how student identities and experiences can enhance the learning experience and improve learning outcomes. This will also include "low floor, high ceiling" instructional strategies that build a ladder to the type of critical thinking learners need to lead, innovate, and break the things that must be broken. Each of these concepts will be broken down with lots of practical examples of what this work looks like in multiple-grade levels and subject areas.

Part IV also discusses common barriers to Tangible Equity and practical ways to overcome these barriers. Some of these barriers will include the fine line between discussing controversy in school without becoming the controversy, strategies to manage pushback from the "politics should not be discussed in the inherently political field of K-12 education" crowd, and prioritizing equity in the face of the system-level "one more thing" syndrome challenges such as budget constraints, leadership changes, and teacher shortages, so educators can "change-proof" Tangible Equity.

By the time you finish this book, you will have several powerful, but practical strategies to make equity real at the classroom level. Because it is not enough to believe, as Dr. Martin Luther King famously said, that "the arc of the moral universe is long, but it bends toward justice."[2] The universe will not bend by itself. It needs a lot of hammering. This kind of work cannot be "one more thing," so the Tangible Equity approach will help educators and families integrate this hammering as a seamless part of what they are already doing.

Whether you teach high school chemistry or third-grade reading intervention, lead a first-grade ELL classroom or lead a school system, support your children at home or support children learning in schools housed in juvenile detention centers, Tangible Equity will give you the tools you need ensure our young people can navigate the unjust system we have while hammering their way to the system we deserve. For too long, we have celebrated the success of young people succeeding through the struggle by successfully playing the game. It's time to start slaying that game so students can get what they need to lead, innovate, and break what must be broken. It's time for Tangible Equity.

Notes

1 NYSED Data Site. n.d. "BRONX HIGH SCHOOL OF SCIENCE ENROLLMENT (2020–21)." https://data.nysed.gov/enrollment.php?instid=800000045625

2 King, Martin Luther, Jr. 2019. "Our God Is Marching On!—The Martin Luther King, Jr, Research and Education Institute." https://kinginstitute.stanford.edu/our-god-marching

1

The Tangible Equity Equation

In the introduction, I defined equity as reducing the predictive power of demographics and zip codes to determine the success of young people inside and outside of the classroom to zero. This utopian idea sounds too pie-in-the-sky for a book called Tangible Equity. But there is a reason I set forward such an extreme, unreachable goal for equity: the process matters more than the outcome.

The Tangible Equity process is part of my personal journey. My story, as a Black child receiving free and reduced lunch from a family of immigrants with an incarcerated father, is one of bucking the highly predictive power of demographics on student success. On demographics alone, I am the type of student our educational system typically does not serve that well. Making matters more complicated, I was not just a bad first grader—I was *gifted* at being bad. I went above and beyond in my mischief. Looking back at my behavior as an adult, I realize that the greatest crimes I committed were not quite the acts of terror they were painted as at the time.

Apparently, I talked. A lot. To everyone. At any time. It did not matter how many days in a row I would lose recess as a punishment, I was going to talk! It is worth noting that taking recess away from a high-energy child is probably going to punish

DOI: 10.4324/9781003282464-3

that teacher post-lunch much more than it punishes the child. I was shocked to learn as an adult that at some point, my mother told my third-grade teacher she was no longer allowed to call her to complain about my unappreciated gift of gab. She couldn't figure out how to stop me from talking either! So deal with it! With the hundreds of keynotes, YouTube videos, podcasts, and panels I speak on each year, maybe talking in class was not really willfully defiant after all.

I was also a repeat offender of the serious felony of excessive question-asking. Because how dare I ask "why" and protest that "it makes no sense" to write the word "paint" ten times when I already knew how to spell it before class even started? My most terrible act? Fighting my teacher. Not fist-fighting or physically attacking my teacher. I'm from a Caribbean family and I learned in pre-school that my family's old-school method of parenting and my highly-sensitive rear end were not compatible, so I was not going to go there. By fighting, I mean having the audacity to question the way a teacher was doing something, or even worse, suggesting that she ought to do that thing my way instead.

As "bad" as these so-called behavior challenges were, they all stemmed from the same root: a lack of being challenged. As you read that last sentence, can you think of a child who shares my story? Behavior challenges arising due to a lack of academic challenges? I want you to personalize this as much as possible because a major event happened in my academic career that can certainly happen for the child you are thinking of right now. That major event was my accidental identification into the New York City Department of Education's gifted and talented program. This was the most transformational experience in my educational career. But you know what the biggest transformation was? The fact that I did not change.

I was still the same Colin. But I was no longer "bad," I was *gifted*. Talking was far less offensive in a class where student-centered work, student-centered inquiry, and basically student-centered everything was simply the way it was. We were the classroom that frequently got that knock from the law-and-order teacher next door about needing to tone it down because her students were almost always at Level 0 (complete silence) while learning. And for some reason, these students then and students I see in classrooms across the country today are often asked to be at Level 0 for all sorts of things that have nothing to do with learning. But that is an issue I will get to later in the book. Another transformation? Asking questions was no longer disrespectful. Asking questions was now *required* for what it meant to be inquisitive and curious. When Mr Eisenberg wanted me to do the required math fair project on fractions with some annoying, unoriginal recipe assignment about multiplying fractional quantities to feed the school what I was certain would be subpar cupcakes, I refused! I told him it was boring, dumb, and I did not want to do it. This would have been a no-recess-for-life moment in another classroom. But for Mr Eisenberg, he was as cool as the other side of the pillow:

Him: "Do you have a better idea?"
Me: "Of course I do! I play piano and I want to do a project called *Fractional Music* where we look at all the ways fractions show up in music with quarter notes, half notes, triplets, dotted quarter notes, etc."
Him: "Class, Colin had a different idea for the math project. Colin, explain what you were saying."
Me: "I am brilliant. Just do what I say because I am brilliant." (paraphrased)
Class (in unison): "Colin is brilliant! Let's just do what he says because he is brilliant."
(100% accurate, word for word)

What could have been a moment of willful defiance in any other classroom became a moment where my advocacy and leadership was encouraged and celebrated. This memory helps me see that I omitted a huge piece of the puzzle in my zealous advocacy for a critical thinking revolution in education. There is a massive prerequisite for critical thinking to flourish in today's education system that is almost entirely an adult issue: ensuring children have the safety to be brilliant. In many of our hyper-compliant, rules-over-everything classroom environments, I question whether these spaces are psychologically safe for students to wonder, ask, speak up, collaborate, offer alternatives, think creatively and do all the things we associate with 21st century readiness.

Culturally, my Caribbean upbringing, like the upbringing of many immigrant households and other super-strict families, was one where "because I said so" was a good-enough justification for parents to do just about anything. But when we think about the safety to be brilliant, do we ever ask ourselves why parent phrases like "don't get smart with me" exist? It is hard for me to think that the grave consequences Black folks could face historically for "getting smart" with the wrong white person does not play a role in this type of rhetoric. I have undocumented family members. So, I am also very familiar with the guidance, said or unsaid, that children of undocumented parents receive about not shining their lights too brightly in school to avoid raising unnecessary attention.

Tangible Equity recognizes that we cannot rest on proclamations and resolutions about how much we care about and value student diversity. It makes no sense to have this beautifully diverse set of students and ask them to spend most of their time conforming to what we deem "normal." There is no value to our students' diversity if we do not find ways to allow them to be themselves as a regularly-scheduled aspect of their learning process.

This resonates with me because I have experienced the downside to what happens when we do not create the psychological and actual safety students need to exercise their brilliance. I lived the student experience of never having a learning space speak to magic of my identity, and I know that I am not alone. My elementary school, self-contained gifted class bussed in some of the most brilliant children from South Brooklyn. But as amazing and transformational as this experience was, I spent years scratching my head about why three of these students did not graduate from high school. Not graduate school, not college, but high school. Mind you, my classmates and I all started high school at least one or two grade levels ahead because of high school credits we earned in middle school. Still, three did not graduate, and I was so close to being the fourth one with the 80 absences I had in ninth grade.

Why does this happen? Why do we have so many children who are rock stars in their earlier grades, but go through this process where the longer they are in school, the less they are into school? I have more questions than answers, and there are plenty of amazing scholars who research this question in more detail. I just know that the painful sight of leaving genius on the table was unbearable for me.

This sight stuck with me when I became a teacher. I was the outcomes-over-everything educator to the extreme. I was not pro-high stakes standardized exams. But I was, and still am, pro-reality. Leveraging Tangible Equity's power must involve interrupting intergenerational poverty. As an educator, therefore, I had to ask myself a simple yes or no question: is education an important part of disrupting intergenerational poverty? Yes or No? Mind you, I'm not asking whether education is the be-all, end-all. But I doubt any reader of this book would doubt whether education was at least an important part of what it takes to interrupt intergenerational poverty.

If we believe this, we must also be able to look into our classrooms and see our students as future doctors, lawyers, engineers, nurses, and even future teachers. This means they have to pass tests. A common objection usually occurs around this time where someone chimes in saying "college isn't for everyone."[1] When we say this, we miss the reality that the power of a thoughtfully financed college degree is undeniably transformational, particularly for women and people of color[2]. Given the vast improvements in earnings with a four-year college degree vs anything less than this, it literally still pays to go to college.[3] But in recognition of the growing opportunities for well-paid, high advancement potential fields that do not require a four-year college degree, we should be clear that tests are still necessary. Plumbers still have to pass tests. So do police officers. We cannot talk about Tangible Equity without talking about the outcomes needed to fulfill the promise of Tangible Equity.

Equity of outcomes sounds utopian. I am often asked, "don't you mean to say equity of opportunity?" The answer is no. I mean to talk about the equity of outcomes. Recall that I am defining equity as reducing the predictive power of demographics on outcomes. This means that changed outcomes are the only way to show that the predictive power of demographics has been reduced. Fortunately, the equity of outcomes is tied to equity in opportunity in significant ways. I would not have received a transformational educational experience had I not been accidentally identified as gifted and bussed to a gifted and talented program outside of my neighborhood. For brilliant students with no such program within bussing distance and without transformational learning options in their neighborhood schools, they do not have this opportunity. But even if they did, opportunity itself would not be enough.

Let's use basketball as an example. Pedro Noguera often uses an example of the National Basketball Association that I want to borrow to explain why opportunity is not enough.[4] In 2020, although Black people represented 13.4% of the population, Black players in the NBA represent 75% of all NBA players.[5] This statistic is often used by doubters, who say "See! Racism and poverty are just excuses. Black athletes' dominance and prominence in basketball proves that if they cared about school as much as they cared about shooting hoops, these inequities would not exist." But Noguera offers brilliant insights to counter this flawed reasoning that uses basketball to teach us what an equity of outcomes could look like in education.

In basketball, the rules are standardized and common to all players. The rim is *always* ten feet off the ground. Basketballs *must* be inflated between 7.5 and 8.5 pounds. The free throw line *has to be* set 15 feet away from the face of the backboard. The point system is standardized and common to all players. A basket in the hoop counts for two points during play. Free throws count as one point. *Anyone* gets three points for shooting the ball from 23′9″ away from the middle of the basket.[6] These rules are the same no matter what state you live in, what basketball court you are playing in, how much money your parents earn, the zip code you live in, your race, your ethnicity, your native language, or your parents' educational level. Basketball, therefore, is a level playing field. The rules of playing the game and the rules for winning the game are always the same. I can therefore conclude that athletically gifted basketball players who do not get injured and put forth the time, effort, and hard work to reach greatness have as much of a shot at NBA success as anyone else with similar situated gifted, healthy, athletes who exert the same time, effort, and hard work.

We are nowhere close to this in education. The only universal standard in the United States' education system is that nothing is universally standard. Outcomes must be tied to opportunity because equitable opportunity is not enough for a brilliant child who is the fourth generation of her family to grow up in an economically disadvantaged trailer park community. She can have a 4.0 grade point average and even be the valedictorian of her class. And even with this impeccable resume, she could still not be accepted to highly selective universities. As outrageous as this might sound, it is even possible that she could graduate at the top of her high school class and not meet the course requirements to enroll in her state's flagship public university. This is not to say merit does not matter, because it does. But merit, alone, is not enough.

When we consider the extraordinary educational effort required to transcend intergenerational poverty, the time, effort, and hard work are not measured by any sort of standardized or common set of rules. Do you remember the wild Varsity Blues scandal that revealed the lengths wealthy families went through to buy their children access to universities through bogus sports accolades, extra-curricular activities, and faked test scores?[7] This illegal scandal pales in comparison with the very legal system that gives the super-privileged access to (and the ability to afford) prestigious unpaid internships, and the pay-to-play social capital system from prestigious pre-kindergarten programs to Ivy League feeder high schools.[8] These are not the same rules. This is not even the same game.

This reality is not news to those growing up in the struggle. Part of why I push so hard for equitable outcomes goes beyond knowing our students need to pass tests to be future doctors, lawyers, engineers, nurses, and even future teachers. Because this is so much more complicated than simply passing tests. As an immigrant, my mother was raised under the mantra that she had to work twice as hard to get half as far. She raised me to understand that as a Black boy growing up in Brooklyn, I was also required to work twice as hard to get half as far. As a father to two young children, I feel completely ashamed that at some point, I need to explain the same thing to my children. I am truly ashamed of myself.

I have dedicated so much of my life to ensuring that stories like mine are no longer the exception to the rule. Yet, I have spent so much of my energy challenging myself to successfully navigate this unfair system instead of challenging the unfair system itself. The rules for playing the game and winning the game are not standardized and common. The rules are highly dependent on what state you live in, what kind of school you go to, how much money your parents earn, the zip code you live in, your race, your ethnicity, your native language, or your parents' educational level.

In education, we are still very far from being able to conclude that academically gifted students growing up in the struggle who put forth the time, effort, and hard work to reach greatness have as much of a shot at successful educational options as anyone else with similar gifts who exert the same time, effort, and hard work. Yet, I have spent so much of my energy helping children master all the tricks and shenanigans of playing an unfair game. What would happen if instead, I focused more on what it would take for them to master the skills needed to slay the game altogether.

Tangible Equity is not an either/or challenge? Academic success must be present for Tangible Equity to exist. But as long as a child's race, income, and zip code translates to requiring extraordinary levels of academic success to reach ordinary outcomes, academic success is not enough. We need academic success and educational justice. Educational justice would mean getting our system to be similar to the standardized and common rules of basketball. The math teacher in me recognized the need for a formula to describe what I am trying to say here in a way that breaks it down more clearly in Figure 1.1.

Think about how often we celebrate stories of children who grow up in the struggle, overcome all sorts of unfair obstacles, and "make it." The Tangible Equity Equation helps us rethink what it means to truly "make it."

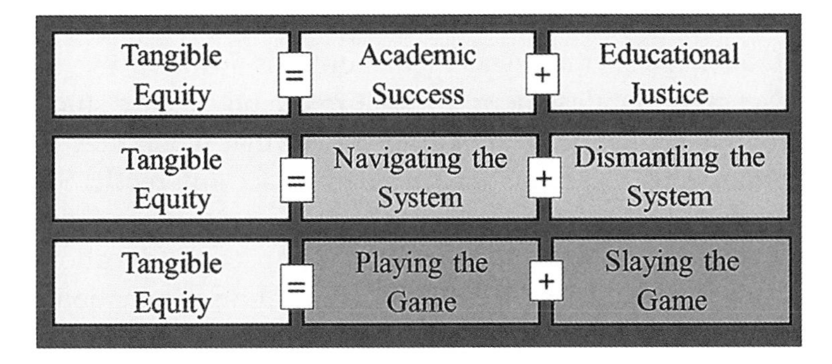

FIGURE 1.1
The Tangible Equity Equation.

I recall my experience as a Computer Science major selected for the amazing INROADS program.[9] This non-profit organization's vision of diversifying Corporate America is 50 years strong, and I was proud to go to New York City and meet lots of other Black and Brown college students aspiring for internships that would put us on the path for lucrative, successful careers in Fortune 500 companies.[10] I remember attending a workshop on how to dress appropriately.

All of us college students had our most professional clothing on, but I only heard what they told us young men because young women received a different workshop. I learned that facial hair was a no-go. I learned that bright-colored shirts underneath my suit were loud and improper. I learned that cornrows were unprofessional. Wearing my hair in twists or locks? Completely unacceptable. I learned how to sit. I learned how to look someone in the eyes and give a firm handshake. How to speak, sit, question, and answer professionally. I could only imagine the kind of lessons the young women learned about how not to dress and how not to style their hair. By the end of the day, I learned the hidden curriculum of how to succeed in Corporate America.

The most important lesson of this hidden curriculum was that important pieces of me needed to stay hidden. The two Black men presenting this workshop were passionate, funny, cool, and caring. They wanted nothing more than to open doors for us, doors that would not be opened if we could not master all the necessary ways-of-being that make these lucrative careers accessible to Black and Brown college students. We had to be "professional." As uneasy as I felt about this, I carried this same mindset into my classroom. I spoke frequently to my students about code-switching so they understood that when they were in "professional" settings they needed to act differently. Speak "properly." Act "appropriately." Because again, if we want to realize the potentially transformational impact of education for students most impacted by the ills of racial discrimination and poverty, access to successful career paths matters.

Something always bothered me about my INROADS experience. If diversity is such an asset to Corporate America,[11] why would they require folks from diverse backgrounds to conform in such an extreme fashion? How could they realize the benefits of my diverse perspective and unique understandings if I am asked to hide so much of myself to even gain access to the entry-level? It is even more bothersome when I realize that I attended this INROADS workshop in the year 2000. In the 20-year period after that workshop, Fortune 500 companies have had only 16 Black CEOs, 36 Latinx CEOs, ten East Asian CEOs, and 22 South Asian CEOs.[12] With only 72 white women holding at the helm during this same time period, leading in Corporate America is still clearly a white man's game.

Again, there is nothing inherently wrong about teaching our young people the hidden curriculum to successfully navigate an unjust system. But at what point do we teach them how to use their access to the system to question it, reimagine it, and dismantle it altogether? From an educational perspective, it is hard to think about classrooms that equip young people with the tools to lead, innovate, and break what needs to be broken when students still get in trouble for asking too many questions. I cannot envision a dismantling of unjust systems when it is still far too common for classroom teachers to punish student leadership and advocacy as "willful defiance."

I understand and value my mother's journey and why working twice as hard to get half as far mattered so much to her life that she had to pass that lesson onto me. I understand and value the journey of the gracious Black men who took a Saturday break from their challenging positions in Corporate America to school us to the tricks we needed to master to access these lucrative career fields. But the work of reducing the impact of demographics on the predictability of outcomes requires that we put equal effort into helping young people know what it takes to play the game as we do equipping them with the transformational tools needed to slay these unjust games altogether.

Notes

1 Rosenbaum, James E. 2017. "OPINION: Stop Driving Kids Crazy—A Four-Year College Degree Isn't the Only Answer." The Hechinger Report. October 17, 2017. https://hechingerreport.org/opinion-stop-driving-kids-crazy-four-year-college-degree-isnt-answer/

2 Seale, Colin. 2019. "The Equity Problem with Saying 'College Isn't for Everyone.'" *Forbes*. May 20, 2019. https://www.forbes.com/sites/colinseale/2019/05/20/the-equity-problem-with-saying-college-isnt-for-everyone/?sh=26e5d19749d0

3 National Center for Education Statistics. 2016. "Digest of Education Statistics, 2017." https://nces.ed.gov/programs/digest/d17/tables/dt17_502.30.asp

4 Noguera, Pedro. 2017. "Excellence through Equity." Presented at the The National Association of ESEA State Program Administrators Conference (formerly the National Title I Association), February 23.

5 Lapchick, Richard, Pedro Ariza, Carter Ellis, Dylan Gladney, Ivan Hudson, David Morrin, Nicholas Mutebi, and Andre Vasquez. 2020. "The 2020 Racial and Gender Report Card: National Basketball Association." https://43530132-36e9-4f52-811a-182c7a91933b.filesusr.com/ugd/7d86e5_9ed7a1185cc8499196117ce9a2c0d050.pdf

6 NBA. 2019. "RULE NO. 1: Court Dimensions—Equipment." February 21, 2019. https://official.nba.com/rule-no-1-court-dimensions-equipment/

7 Pascus, Brian. 2019. "Operation Varsity Blues List: Every Charge, Plea and Accusation Facing the Parents in the College Admissions Scandal." March 13, 2019. https://www.cbsnews.com/news/college-admissions-scandal-list-operation-varsity-blues-every-charge-plea-accusation-facing-parents-2019-05-16/

8 Gregory, Sean. 2021. "As Varsity Blues Trails Start, College Sports Still Unequal." *Time*. September 27, 2021. https://time.com/6100715/varsity-blues-trial-college-sports/

9 Inroads. 2019. "Inroads: The Network You Need to Go Where You Want." https://inroads.org/about-inroads/history-mission/
10 Inroads. 2020. "INROADS Report to the Community—Fiscal Years 2019–2020." Issuu. https://issuu.com/inroadsinc/docs/community_report_final_web_version/2
11 Hunt, Vivian, Dennis Layton, and Sara Prince. 2015. "Why Diversity Matters." McKinsey & Company. January 1, 2015. https://www.mckinsey.com/business-functions/organization/our-insights/why-diversity-matters
12 The Society Pages. 2020. "Fortune 500 CEOs, 2000–2020: Still Male, Still White." *The Society Pages*. October 28, 2020. https://thesocietypages.org/specials/fortune-500-ceos-2000-2020-still-male-still-white/

Bibliography

Gregory, Sean. 2021. "As Varsity Blues Trails Start, College Sports Still Unequal." *Time*. September 27, 2021. https://time.com/6100715/varsity-blues-trial-college-sports/

Hunt, Vivian, Dennis Layton, and Sara Prince. 2015. "Why Diversity Matters." McKinsey & Company. January 1, 2015. https://www.mckinsey.com/business-functions/organization/our-insights/why-diversity-matters

Inroads. 2019. "Inroads: The Network You Need to Go Where You Want." https://inroads.org/about-inroads/history-mission/

Inroads. 2020. "INROADS Report to the Community—Fiscal Years 2019–2020." Issuu. https://issuu.com/inroadsinc/docs/community_report_final_web_version/2

King, Martin Luther, Jr. 2019. "Our God Is Marching On!—The Martin Luther King, Jr, Research and Education Institute." *Stanford.edu*. 2019. https://kinginstitute.stanford.edu/our-god-marching

Lapchick, Richard, Pedro Ariza, Carter Ellis, Dylan Gladney, Ivan Hudson, David Morrin, Nicholas Mutebi, and Andre Vasquez. 2020. "The 2020 Racial and Gender Report Card: National Basketball Association." https://43530132-36e9-4f52-811a-182c7a91933b.filesusr.com/ugd/7d86e5_9ed7a1185cc8499196117ce9a2c0d050.pdf

NBA. 2019. "RULE NO. 1: Court Dimensions—Equipment." February 21, 2019. https://official.nba.com/rule-no-1-court-dimensions-equipment/

NIH. n.d. "Implicit Bias." https://diversity.nih.gov/sociocultural-factors/implicit-bias

Pascus, Brian. 2019. "Operation Varsity Blues List: Every Charge, Plea and Accusation Facing the Parents in the College Admissions Scandal." March 13, 2019. https://www.cbsnews.com/news/college-admissions-scandal-list-operation-varsity-blues-every-charge-plea-accusation-facing-parents-2019-05-16/

Rosenbaum, James E. 2017. "OPINION: Stop Driving Kids Crazy—A Four-Year College Degree Isn't the Only Answer." *The Hechinger Report*. October 17, 2017. https://hechingerreport.org/opinion-stop-driving-kids-crazy-four-year-college-degree-isnt-answer/

Seale, Colin. 2019. "The Equity Problem with Saying 'College Isn't for Everyone.'" *Forbes*. May 20, 2019. https://www.forbes.com/sites/colinseale/2019/05/20/the-equity-problem-with-saying-college-isnt-for-everyone/?sh=26e5d19749d0

The Society Pages. 2020. "Fortune 500 CEOs, 2000–2020: Still Male, Still White." *The Society Pages*. October 28, 2020. https://thesocietypages.org/specials/fortune-500-ceos-2000-2020-still-male-still-white/

2

Beyond the Buzzwords

One of the many valid criticisms of standardized exams is that they ask questions no-one would ever ask in real-life. If you told a colleague that you had just finished reading the first couple of chapters from the brilliant, amazingly handsome author of this book, no colleague would ever respond with, "Really? What is the main idea of the book so far?" But just in case that conversation did come up, you should know that the main idea of this book is that teachers need practical tools to support Tangible Equity at the classroom level. The "how" is the point. We just cannot get to the "how" just yet.

Change fatigue is ubiquitous in education. Getting past this change fatigue and agreeing to change as an initial step can feel like moving mountains. Continuing the momentum of change in the face of competing priorities, leadership turnover, and the wild day-to-day realities of being an educator can feel like mission impossible. But the mission is inherently more possible when there is a deep commitment to the mission itself. Getting to the "why" is a crucial part of establishing this commitment.

Getting to the "why" for Tangible Equity requires going beyond buzzwords. This is not to say we should ignore the significant ways education issues involving diversity, equity, inclusion, anti-racism, White Privilege, and systemic rac-

DOI: 10.4324/9781003282464-4

ism feed into the power of demographic predictability. But the typical remedy of the equity checklist is not going to be sufficient.

For instance, districts often kickoff their equity work with extensive training on implicit bias. I understand why, because although few teachers would admit to being outright racist or discriminatory towards certain groups of students, it is challenging to explain the predictive power of demographics on academic outcomes without presuming some type of bias is involved. Implicit bias is the blanket term for the type of conduct associated with attitudes and actions based on those attitudes that stem from stereotypes.[1] And this is often referred to as implicit bias because, supposedly, this conduct is not happening within the realm of our conscious knowledge.

I hate the term implicit bias and I think it needs to be retired, immediately. How can "bias occurring outside of the realm of conscious knowledge" be blamed when a police officer decides to shoot Jacob Blake in his back seven times as he was heading back into his vehicle where his children were? Was implicit bias some sort of hidden factor behind Derek Chauvin's decision to press his knee against George Floyd's neck for eight minutes and 46 seconds? What about his three colleagues who stood there, indifferent to George Floyd's pleas for life, reminders that he could not breath, and cries for his mother? Is this reckless disregard for human life some sort of subconscious, "I had no clue what I was doing," phenomenon?

Beyond policing, how can implicit bias explain why so-called "ethnic-sounding names" get called in for interviews less than the same level of experience?[2] In housing, do you really think implicit bias is the justification for why the appraised values for homes are lower when Black people have lived in those homes?[3] Can we look at the tremendously stubborn gifted gap and blame implicit bias in the face of a study by Vanderbilt University professors that found that even with identical test scores, white students were twice as likely as Black students to be selected for gifted programs?[4]

This is raw, in-your-face, explicit bias. Why are we so afraid to call explicit bias out for what it is? I am not entirely sure of why the term implicit bias has become so popular, even by experts who fully understand how the ills of racism lead to explicit, in-your-face, acts of domestic terrorism, the pushing out of Black girls in schools, the demonization of immigrant families and children, and countless acts of soul-crushing experiences students of color face in our school systems.

If I had to guess, I would presume that implicit bias just sounds better. It just feels a little bit safer. "I'm not a bad person, I just have implicit bias issues. Who doesn't?" This cannot suffice. If we truly wish to engage in the honest, open, and self-reflective work needed to combat racism at an individual and systemic level, we must acknowledge that "implicit bias" is letting us off the hook.

If we cannot explicitly name how explicit bias impacts our conduct, racial justice will remain illusory. The time for retiring the phrase "implicit bias" as the excuse for deplorable, racist conduct is long overdue. What we should be asking ourselves instead is how are we explicitly biased and what are we going to do to change this?

Going further down the equity checklist, one-and-done workshops on concepts like culturally responsive pedagogy, restorative justice, diverse book selection, and trauma-informed education do not get us to Tangible Equity either. When a math teacher creates a problem about Tyrone shopping for Kwanzaa supplies or Juliana buying decorations for her quinceañera, these surface level changes do not truly activate the compelling connection between student, content, and reality that unleashes the critical thinking benefits of true culturally responsive approach.

Similarly, restorative practices cannot just be a strategy for reactively addressing discipline issues. Restorative practices must be a proactive instructional approach that uses instruction to restore our students' learning experiences by rehumanizing content. Diverse books are important. But it is also important that do not limit the possibilities your fourth-grade soccer star from Honduras by presuming she needs to read the story about the Latina soccer prodigy instead of the story about the white male skiing sensation. Because maybe that skiing story about hard work and perseverance was written in a way where she could make a connection and possibly launch a pathway to be an Olympic skier herself.

One of the most misunderstood concepts discussed in most equity conversations is the idea of trauma-informed education. Every new school year, for example, a social media post warning about "How I spent my summer vacation" tends to go viral. This post asks teachers to avoid this type of assignment for fear that it can traumatize some students and make them feel less than. The thinking is, students who are already dealing with a lot of trauma may get further traumatized if some students spent their summer vacations in Europe while others spent summer vacation hanging out with abuela. I understand the sentiment behind this type of paternalistic thinking. But who are we to decide which stories have value? I believe our world would be a better place if my students who spent their summers traveling the world knew about the magic of summers with abuela.

We know that the tough situations our students face have a real impact on student achievement. Knowledge of Adverse Childhood Experiences (ACES) are increasingly a focus of school systems looking to give educators the requisite empathy and understanding to serve all children.[5] But so often, if focusing too much on the trauma hurts children even more. Whether we want to call it Mother Theresa syndrome or Pobrecito syndrome,[6] educators sometimes believe that because some children have it so tough in life, we should excuse their academic struggles in school and lower our expectations.[7] This is a guaranteed way to continue to traumatize our children. Especially because this notion ignores the fact that when our young people are living through the struggle and become successful, this success doesn't occur despite all their pain and suffering in life. It happens because of it.

In the following chapter, I explain why Tangible Equity requires us to continuously reflect on the ways our biases, even if well-intentioned, can be harmful to students. When it comes to trauma-informed education, we need to constantly remind ourselves that as educators, we typically have stable, middle-class jobs with decent benefits. Even if our origin stories involve struggle that helps us relate to struggles students may be enduring, we are now in a different chapter. Educators have to remind themselves that a lot of what we call "trauma," our students call "Tuesday." This does not mean we teach without empathy. It is actually the opposite. Educators need to balance the dual reality that today's schools must work miracles to overcome out-of-school challenges *and* ensure we do not traumatize students even further by denying them access to the transformational educational experiences they need.

Notes

1 NIH. n.d. "Implicit Bias." https://diversity.nih.gov/sociocultural-factors/implicit-bias
Implicit bias is a form of bias that occurs automatically and unintentionally, that nevertheless affects judgments, decisions, and behaviors. Research has shown implicit bias can pose a barrier to recruiting and retaining a diverse scientific workforce.
2 Gerdeman, Dina. 2017. "Minorities Who 'Whiten' Job Resumes Get More Interviews." HBS Working Knowledge. *Harvard Business School*. May 17, 2017. https://hbswk.hbs.edu/item/minorities-who-whiten-job-resumes-get-more-interviews
3 Kamin, Debra. 2020. "Black Homeowners Face Discrimination in Appraisals." *The New York Times*. August 27, 2020, sec. Real Estate. https://www.nytimes.com/2020/08/25/realestate/blacks-minorities-appraisals-discrimination.html
4 Grissom, Jason A., and Christopher Redding. 2016. "Discretion and Disproportionality." *AERA Open* 2, no. 1. https://doi.org/10.1177/2332858415622175
5 CDC. 2020. "About the CDC-Kaiser ACE Study—Violence Prevention." September 3, 2020. https://www.cdc.gov/violenceprevention/aces/about.html?CDC_AA_refVal=https%3A%2F%2Fwww.cdc.gov%2Fviolenceprevention%2Facestudy%2Fabout.html
6 Cepeda, Esther J. 2013. "Cepeda: In Education, a 'Pobrecito' Syndrome." *The Salt Lake Tribune*. August 10, 2013. https://archive.sltrib.com/article.php?id=56717963&itype=CMSID

7 Alverio, Diane. 2013. "Opinion: Not All Minority Children Are Disadvantaged or at Risk." *CTLN*. November 4, 2013. https://ctlatinonews.com/opinion-demolishing-stereotypes/

Bibliography

Alverio, Diane. 2013. "Opinion: Not All Minority Children Are Disadvantaged or at Risk." *CTLN*. November 4, 2013. https://ctlatinonews.com/opinion-demolishing-stereotypes/

CDC. 2020. "About the CDC-Kaiser ACE Study—Violence Prevention." September 3, 2020. https://www.cdc.gov/violenceprevention/aces/about.html?CDC_AA_refVal=https%3A%2F%2Fwww.cdc.gov%2Fviolenceprevention%2Facestudy%2Fabout.html

Cepeda, Esther J. 2013. "Cepeda: In Education, a 'Pobrecito' Syndrome." *The Salt Lake Tribune*. August 10, 2013. https://archive.sltrib.com/article.php?id=56717963&itype=CMSID

Gerdeman, Dina. 2017. "Minorities Who 'Whiten' Job Resumes Get More Interviews." HBS Working Knowledge. *Harvard Business School*. May 17, 2017. https://hbswk.hbs.edu/item/minorities-who-whiten-job-resumes-get-more-interviews

Grissom, Jason A., and Christopher Redding. 2016. "Discretion and Disproportionality." *AERA Open* 2, no 1. https://doi.org/10.1177/2332858415622175

Kamin, Debra. 2020. "Black Homeowners Face Discrimination in Appraisals." *The New York Times*. August 27, 2020. sec. Real Estate. https://www.nytimes.com/2020/08/25/realestate/blacks-minorities-appraisals-discrimination.html

3

The Case for Tangible Equity

I smile when I think about the strong likelihood that the Venn diagram for those who feel there is no place for politics in school, believe that schools should teach about the history of the United States in the most favorable light possible, advocate for American Exceptionalism, and praise our nation's Founding Fathers is a circle. Interestingly, I doubt that folks in this circle ever view patriotism as a radical act of love that demands that we live up to our creed. This surprises me because our Founding Fathers were mostly young revolutionaries who violently overthrew a government they believed was unjust.

Because I know a strong "why" is needed to commit to the Tangible Equity change process, I want to view the historical and now case from this patriotic lens. Making this case does not require me to use and define the highly complex, yet often oversimplified terms like White Privilege and systemic racism that trigger predicable backlash from some audiences. The case for Tangible Equity merely requires me to conjure up the very deep sense of patriotism I feel as a first-generation immigrant who still gets goosebumps when a singer performs The Star-Spangled Banner and ends with this powerful questions: "O say does that Star-Spangled Banner yet wave o'er the land of the free and the home of the brave?" This two-part inquiry is the most power-

DOI: 10.4324/9781003282464-5

ful pair of questions asked in the history of the United States of America, and these are what guide my case for Tangible Equity. Is this the land of the free? Is this the home of the brave?

Freedom and bravery. Certainly, there is nothing anti-American about pondering notions of freedom and bravery, right? Recall that the equity definition used in this book is all about reducing the predictive power of demographics on outcomes. By the end of this chapter, you will understand the origin story of this predictive power with much more clarity. Analyzing the historical record and the number of overlapping trends between the historical record and today's data helps to explain why the Tangible Equity approach is necessary.

In an 18-month span, I scoured data for over 50 school systems to make the local case for Tangible Equity as part of preparing for educator workshops. The patterns were eye-opening. I always start my workshops on Tangible Equity by looking at maps showing where our community schools are located, whether I'm in Detroit, Chicago, El Paso, Richmond, Brooklyn, Springfield (Missouri or Illinois), Louisville, or Seattle. Then, I pull up maps showing neighborhoods with the highest Black and Latinx concentrations. Even in smaller towns with less diverse populations, there is almost always an interesting divide based on socioeconomic status: the other side of the tracks, up the hill, east of the interstate, etc.

When I pull up these maps and look at data tracked by zip codes and census tracts, troubling patterns emerge. The predictability of outcomes based on demographics is usually off the charts. As a clarifying point, just because there are very real struggles in these communities does not mean we ignore the positives. Neighborhoods with these challenges still have lots of magic, treasure, joy, celebration, history, community, and love. But we cannot talk about Tangible Equity without understanding why the "heat" maps that show the greatest crime rates and the lowest high school graduation rates look just like the racial concentration maps. Or how the highest infant mortality rates and lowest access to broadband internet at home often match almost exactly, the same racial concentration maps. I felt like I was punched in the gut when I learned that in Albany, NY, four out of five non-white residents could not buy high-fiber bread or low-fat milk in their neighborhoods and that living in a low-income neighborhood in Baltimore—neighborhoods that correspond heavily to the same racial concentration maps—makes you more than three times more likely to lack access to healthy food options.

The New Deal or a Raw Deal?

History helps us understand why these patterns are so powerful, especially when we question these patterns by asking whether this is truly the land of the free and the home of the brave. One of the most significant examples of the predictive power of demographics as destiny is the stubborn racial wealth gap. On average, for every dollar in wealth, Black and Latinx folks have 12 cents and 21 cents, respectively.[1] History helps us understand why these patterns are so powerful, especially when we question these patterns by asking whether the United States is truly the land of the free and the home of the brave. From that lens, it is unquestionable that World War II veterans put forth a tremendous amount of bravery to fight for freedom abroad. When the New Deal passed, it was therefore not surprising that the United States would want to reward our veterans for their incredible sacrifices.

What we do not typically learn in the standard US History curriculum, however, is that this New Deal felt more like a raw deal to Black veterans returning from the war. For no other reason but the color of their skin, Black veterans were excluded from the benefits of the GI Bill. Even though they were not explicitly carved out of this massive package of benefits, you could not access these benefits, period, if you did not receive an honorable discharge. Racism prevented a lot of Black veterans from receiving these benefits. Even when they did, vocational education programs paid for by the GI Bill excluded Blacks from more lucrative fields like plumbing and other high-paying trades.

When openly racist members of Congress, especially in Southern states, worried that the dignity and honor that veterans rightfully deserved may result in Black veterans receiving improved treatment, they sought to exclude Blacks from the GI bill altogether. But, because that was not politically tenable, Congress was able to leverage the often-problematic use of "state rights" to allow states to administer GI Bill benefits in race-exclusionary ways.[2]

The connection between history and today does not end there. I am imperfect in many ways, but one of my biggest imperfections is my habit of judging something or someone without appropriate context. For instance, the first time saw someone holding up a sign on a street corner advertising a car wash to pay for funeral expenses of a relative, I shook my head. What is wrong with these people? Why can't these people simply get a life insurance policy? It frustrated me even more once when I noticed that almost every person I saw doing this was Black or Latinx. My frustration cooled, considerably, when I realized part of the reason why these people, who seemed so brave in their approach to use entrepreneurial ways to pay for burial expenses, couldn't simply get a life insurance policy. Insurance companies, historically, lobbied states for race-based exclusions to coverage and used race as a factor to raise premiums so high that life insurance would be impractical.[3] This contributed to the wealth gap between whites and non-whites in the United States, therefore, because working white families of average means were able to pass on wealth to their families through life insurance while non-white families were not.

Before I go further, I want to name the defensive emotion some readers might start to feel right now. Why does it always have to be about race? Shouldn't there be a statute of limitations on claims of historical racism? I thought this book was supposed to be about practical classroom strategies for reducing the predictive power of demographics, not this preachy, race-baiting, super "woke" stuff that should make white people feel ashamed of their ancestors.

I want to share that I once held a very similar critique, and perhaps my critique was far more harsh: who cares? Seriously, I felt like I am teaching students today, in my school today, in their community today, and the only thing that matters to me is this magic moment where I have the opportunity to give students the instruction they need to navigate through today regardless of what happened yesterday. I ask you to think about holding this tension close and following the advice from my first book, *Thinking Like a Lawyer: A Framework for Teaching Critical Thinking to All Students*, where I speak about the equity case for pushing through this tension:

> The simple exercise of developing a plausible argument for a side you do not agree with is a powerful tool. The ability to put oneself in the shoes of others to experience a conflict from their point of view is the essence of empathy.

So please, allow me some more space to provide additional historical context on why the "why" for Tangible Equity's push to reduce the predictive power of demographics of outcomes is so important.

The Rural South

Back to the maps, one particular map always causes me to scratch my head a bit. During every recent election, maps showing the racial demographics and voting patterns of Rural America go viral. From a land mass perspective, it appears that if land voted instead of people, the favorite presidential candidate of Rural America would win by a landslide. But there is an interesting demographic characteristic of the people who inhabit this land: only one out of every five people living in Rural America is non-white. I wish I was not hard-wired to go full-scale investigative journalist on everything that intrigues me, but I am who I am.

How did Rural America come to be so overwhelmingly white? Without question, the freedom and bravery questions of our national anthem extend to the long-suffering enslaved folks who labored without pay until their emancipation. And the historical records are very clear in showing that Blacks, particularly for Southern states where slavery proliferated, lived and labored predominantly in rural areas.

Today's Rural America demographics might make this hard to believe and even harder to understand, but in 1900, nine out of every ten Blacks lived in the South and three out of every four lived on farms. During the Great Migration that occurred between 1910 and 1970, six million Blacks left the South.[4] Growing up with New York City winters, experiencing knee-shaking winds in Chicago, and living through the awful lake effect snow of Syracuse that is similar to weather patterns in Midwest states bordering the Great Lakes left me with my biggest question: why would anybody choose to live in the cold on purpose? I know this first-hand because my choice to live in the deserts of Las Vegas and Phoenix for the last 15 years was not a choice, it was an escape!

But back to the maps, why would all these Black people leave? In 1920, there were over 900,000 Black farmers, and over half of all Black people in America lived on farms. Then, Black farmers accounted for 14% of the nation's farmers. Today, less than 50,000, or 1.3% of farmers are Black.[5] It is hard to comprehend how we go from half of the nation's Black population living on farms to having your racial identity as a Black person becoming a solid predictor of whether you have access to healthy food options in your neighborhood. But putting that aside, history shows us that Rural America's massive transformation to an overwhelmingly white majority did not occur by accident. It happened because it is pretty hard to survive, much less thrive, in Rural America without land.

The story of the Great Migration of six million Blacks leaving the South cannot be told without the story of the dispossession of 12 million acres of land owned by Black farmers over the last century. The New Deal, yet again, was a raw deal for Black farmers who did not benefit from various legislation meant to prop up struggling farms. Certainly, emancipation gave more credence to the question of whether the United States is the land of the free. But given that the economic value of enslaved human beings at the time of the Civil War exceeded the value of our nation's railroads and factories combined,[6] it seems odd to not provide any money, land, clothes, housing, or food to freed Blacks whose labor created all this value. One might suggest that "home of the brave" justifications matter here, because it's supposedly the American way to pull yourself up from your own bootstraps.

Under this bootstrap mindset, it becomes easy to downplay the famously broken promise of 40 acres and a mule. General William Tecumseh Sherman's January 1865 Special Field Order 15 set aside 400,000 acres of former Confederate land for newly-freed Blacks to farm. After 40,000 freedmen settled on this land, the General gave the army permission to loan the new settlers mules. After Lincoln's assassination, President Andrew Johnson swiftly overturned this order and returned this land to its former Confederate owners.[7] Then and now, the anti-handout mentality can easily be squared with the idea that rewards are a result of hard work and effort. Never mind that there were no financial rewards, period, or the unpaid slave labor that transformed the United States into a global economic superpower.

But what happens when all handouts are not equally frowned-upon? 40,000 former enslaved Black people scurried to have access to 40 acres of land after a lifetime of unpaid labor. On the other hand, for the cost of a small filing fee, almost 1.5 million white families benefited from receiving 160-acre tracts of federal land under the citizens-only Homestead Act that was not available to freed Blacks (who were not eligible to be considered citizens of the United States at that time).

There are at least four significant ramifications of this government sponsored, whites-only, handout. First, by practically giving away 10% of all land owned by the United States, this was by far the most significant handout in United States history. Second, these lands, in many cases, were the sovereign lands of Native Americans that were not the property of the United States to offer to begin with. Third, this helps to explain the overwhelmingly white population of the rural land settled during our nation's Westward Expansion. Lastly, the aftermath of this Act provides one of the most compelling pieces of evidence explaining the 100-plus year head start Blacks are trying to catch up on given our nation's wealth gap: almost 46 million adults in the United States today—almost 20% of our adult population—descend from beneficiaries of these homesteaders.

The miraculous demographic shift of Rural America is not miraculous at all. It is a predictable result of explicit policy choices. Jim Crow laws, race-based massacres of thriving Black communities like Roswell and Greenfield, and the everyday dehumanization of having no choice but to use separate and worse facilities, services, and opportunities certainly played a huge role in The Great Migration and today's rural demographics. Unpleasant people are one thing. But untenable policies are another.

Legislation like the Agricultural Adjustment Act[8] that compensated struggling farmers during a time of immense losses and forced crop reductions sounded great, in theory. In practice, congressional leadership gave into pressures from Jim Crow politicians by allowing the economic benefits to be administered at the local levels, where Black farmers were all-but-guaranteed to not receive these benefits.[9] The long-documented discriminatory practices of the United States Department of Agriculture when it comes to unfairly denying Black farmers access to loans adds to this predictable phenomenon.[10] Modern farming is impossible without access to credit needed to stave off seasonal and weather-related farming challenges and purchase the expensive equipment needed to modernize farms. Tangible Equity requires the type of reflective instinct to investigate the story whenever it appears that race or other demographics seem to play too heavy of a role in phenomenon. Getting to today's map of racial demographics in Rural America from the reality in 1900, where nine out of every ten Blacks lived in the South and three out of every four lived on farms, requires a committed effort to test our history against those same two questions: is this the land of the free? Is this the home of the brave?

This chapter started with questions about the uncomfortable role demographics play in the predictability of outcomes. So many of the examples provided discuss involve wealth because wealth is still one of the most important measures of well-being in the United States. If I stopped here, it would be safe to presume that the South was just a bad place for Black people and that all things shifted to the good when Black folks moved up north to industrial regions. As you might predict, this was not the case.

Escaping Racism for More Racism

Freedom meant little to Black folks who moved North, but could not penetrate whites-only labor unions. Blacks from Mississippi and Louisiana who came West to build the highly treacherous Hoover Dam in Nevada were certainly brave, but their race—not their bravery—was what subjected them to substandard wages and housing accommodations. Even the freedom to move, period, was not a freedom afforded to Blacks. With Blacks regularly facing exclusion, humiliation, and violence on buses and trains, the growth of automobile transport was a welcome liberation. But for Black people, it turned out that "getting your kicks on Route 66" meant getting kicked around and getting kicked out.

2019's acclaimed movie, The Green Book, made popular the history of The Negro Motorist Green Book.[11] This must-have resource for the Black driver helped "The Negro" traveling by car navigate racism on the road by sharing safe places "that will keep him from running into difficulties, embarrassments and to make his trip more enjoyable." The history of Sundown Towns—communities where Blacks were not allowed to be after sunset—prove that the Midwest, Northeast, Mountain, and West coast were not safe havens against racial terrorism that was more commonly associated with southern states during this time.[12]

Home Ownership and The Wealth Gap

In my final reference to maps, I want to highlight one last example of how benefits of the New Deal meant to lift the nation out of the Great Depression explicitly contributed to the role demographics play in predictability of outcomes that we see today. Encouraging home ownership as a pathway to wealth and prosperity was a no-brainer. Buy a home with an affordable interest rate, you have an asset. You can use this asset to take out a loan and start a business, build more wealth. You can pay off your home and pass down a paid-off home to your children, giving them a significant head start in their adult life.

The creation of The Homeowner's Loan Corporation (HOLC),[13] a precursor to the Federal Housing Administration's loan-backing program, was therefore an extremely logical policy choice to lift the nation out of its financial crisis. The benefit of government-backed loans was a boon to skeptical lenders who were burned with the huge stock market crash of 1929, but were now assured payback with the full trust and faith of the United States government. That said, loans still could not be administered without some level of scrutiny.

As expected, this scrutiny ended up being another clear example of how the mass home ownership campaign of the New Deal was also a raw deal for non-whites. The HOLC did not grant loans in communities formally labeled "hazardous." These areas received a D-rating on maps prepared by loan officers. For easier viewing, the D-rated areas were colored in with red highlights, as a clear indicator that no government-backed loans would be available to anyone in these communities. This is the origin of the term redlining, and to understand why loan officers deemed certain communities hazardous with a D-rating, or labeled others as "definitely declining" with a C-rating is to understand the formal, policy and practice-based modern history of racial discrimination in the United States.[14]

Look at the South Oak Cliff community of Dallas, Texas today. This area, as I mentioned earlier when I described other struggling communities, has no shortage of love, joy, magic, treasure, history, brilliance, and community. But this area—which was and still is predominately populated by Blacks—is also home to the zip codes with the highest incarceration rate in Texas and the wrong side of so many other important measures of well-being.[15] Imagine looking at this area about 100 years ago, observing vacant property on each side, noticing level terrain, and real estate's most cliché phrase: location, location, location, also holds true. You see lots of schools and stores in the area and know that the neighborhood boasts lots of city conveniences. And even though transportation is not great, even though there are some unpaved streets, and even though this neighborhood is quite far from the major business centers of Dallas, you also know that a new Coca Cola Plant is about to be built just south of there. How could you conclude, as the official indicated in the HOLC notes for this community, that "[v]ery little likelihood of any chance in the area in the near future."[16]

Practicing the Tangible Equity reflection mindset forces a deeper level of questioning. Why would a community with so many inherent assets be written off so coldly? It turns out, the fatal flaw of the South Oak Cliff community at this time was its Black inhabitants. In El Paso, redlined border communities were denied access to wealth because of the "Mexican peons" who lived there. In Kansas City, Missouri, Tacoma, Washington, and elsewhere, the presence of Belgian, Irish, Italian, Polish, and Eastern European were similarly doomed. This, despite one area of Tacoma being labeled the "Melting Pot" district in a nation that taught me, and likely taught you, that the "Melting Pot" was a defining feature of what made our country great. I say that these foreign groups were similarly doomed because the impact of redlining was not the same for many of these communities over time.

Redlining was standard practice well into the 1970s when housing discrimination laws started to be enforced. And although I recognize that as a first-generation immigrant myself, some level of assimilation is expected, I also prefer the metaphor of immigration-spurred diversity as a tossed salad over the idea of melting into a pot and disappearing into the stew. That said, being Black or of Asian or Hispanic descent made it a lot harder to melt into the pot than it was for European immigrants to. In one or two generations, a family of European immigrants could change their last name, lose their accents, and receive the highly valuable recognition and rewards of being considered white. One of the more fascinating examples of this journey is the story of Italian Americans fighting hard to have Christopher Columbus recognized with a national holiday.[17] Without discussing the questionable legacy of Columbus and the scope of the genocide committed during his voyages, the struggle of Italians Americans to be seen as "real" Americans—and the concept of "real" Americans, period—cannot be separated from the tangible value of whiteness.

It is heartbreaking to see that the maps of redlined communities from almost 100 years ago are shockingly accurate predictors of the struggles in today's maps. My neighborhood in Phoenix, Arizona was redlined because our occupants were "largely Mexicans, Negroes, and the lower classes of white working people." And this same community today has some of the highest poverty rates, lowest median incomes, and had one of the highest rates of COVID-19 related deaths than anywhere else in the Phoenix metropolitan area.

Anyone with a healthy sense of skepticism will start to throw up all sorts of red flags and question marks right now. Two questions, in particular, speak to the level of doubt I have about the inevitability of the outcomes we see today based on decisions made by loan officers way back when. First, I grew up watching The Jeffersons. This show was all about a Black family who, through hard work and perseverance, were able to move on up to the East Side to a deluxe apartment in the sky because they've finally got a piece of the pie. So, my skeptical position is this: if George and Weezie could "move on up" out of the type of redlined communities depicted in the maps, it must have been the fault of Black folks who were not willing to work hard enough to do the same.

I was surprised to find the answers I was looking for in the memory bank I keep from my middle school theater class. If I told you that my almost entirely Black school read and performed scenes from a play written by a Black playwright featuring an almost Black cast, you would have a 50/50 shot of being right if you picked August Wilson's *Fences* or Lorraine Hansberry's *A Raisin in the Sun*. We actually did both! But the best response to the "why didn't Blacks and other redlined groups simply move on up question" comes from Hansberry's classic work.

A Raisin in the Sun tells the moving story of the Youngers—a hard-working Black family whose patriarch died after accomplishing the rare feat of leaving a fully-paid life insurance policy that the insurance company actually honored. His survivors attempted to tackle the even rarer feat of being able to "move on up" out of the South Side of Chicago in a nice, safe, white neighborhood. This was a textbook example of a Black family doing all the things to "move on up" and ending up with their hopes and dreams crushed.[18]

Facing financial pressure after a failed business venture, the protagonist Walter Lee strongly considers giving into a kinder, gentler type of discrimination that merely sought to pay the Younger family for not moving in to avoid shaking up the natural order of things. The play ends with Walter Lee's heartwarming reversal, where he talks through the proud history of his family's history in this country. Explains that he works hard as a chauffeur and his wife works hard as a domestic laborer. Explains that his father once almost beat a man to death because he called him a bad name. Explains that he is from proud people, and he is proud that his little sister is going to be a doctor. And after pulling his son close to him, he tells the white representative from the homeowner's association that came to finalize the payoff that they changed their mind: they are going to move into the house after all because in Walter Lee's words, "my father—my father—he earned it for us brick by brick" (Hansberry, Act 3).

His courage to move in despite the risks moves me to tears every time I read the play or watch Sidney Poitier's epic portrayal of Walter Lee in the classic film version. But I just said that this was a classic story of what happens when hard-working Black folks do everything they are asked, work hard, persevere, and still end up getting their hopes and dreams crushed. This story had a happily-ever-after, God bless America, maybe this is truly the land of the free and the home of the brave type of ending. Something never sat right with me about this ending, however. Right before the white representative from the homeowner's association leaves, he scurries off the stage with the main characters focused intently on Walter Lee until the moment the door is closed and they can begin their celebration. His last lines to the Younger family were too ominous for me to ignore:

> Well—if you are that final about it ... there is nothing left for me to say. I sure hope you people know what you're getting into.
>
> (Hansberry, Act 3)

My spider sense for bad things about to go down is a natural byproduct of growing up how I grew up in Brooklyn.

If someone told me or my family as their last words before I decide to move into a mostly white neighborhood something like "I sure hope you people know what you're getting into," I would not view that as a threat. I would view it as a promise! In Lorraine Hansberry's original version of the play submitted to her publisher, this ominous warning ended up serving as a clear example of foreshadowing. In an interview, Hansberry left no doubts of her feelings about the Younger family's future when she responded to a question about a reviewer who saw this as warm and fuzzy ending: "If he thinks that's a happy ending, I invite him to come live in one of the communities where the Youngers are going!"[19]

Hansberry was so troubled by the happily-ever-after reception of the mostly white audiences who made *Raisin* a smashing success that she released an updated version of the play that included omitted scenes.[20] One omitted scene involved a child, Travis Younger, telling his mother about how much fun he and his friends had playing a game of "catch the rat." Another omitted scene involved a detailed conversation between the Lena Younger, the family matriarch and the neighborhood gossip, Mrs Johnson. Knowing that the Younger family was getting ready to move into the mostly-white neighborhood of Clybourne Park, Mrs Johnson is surprised that Lena "ain't read 'bout them colored people who were bombed out of their place out there." Later in this scene, Mrs Johnson predicts what the newspaper headlines will read one month after the Youngers move in. "Lord I bet this time next month y'all names will have been in the papers plenty: 'NEGROES INVADE CLYBOURNE PARK BOMBED!'"

The complexity of "moving on up" was personal to Lorraine Hansberry because her father, Carl Hansberry was the lead plaintiff in *Hansberry v. Lee*, one of the key Supreme Court cases that made racially restrictive covenants unconstitutional.[21] Restrictive covenants are just a fancy way to say if you live here, you agree to certain levels of community standards. Homeowner's associations have a ton of restrictive covenants. I cannot paint my house zebra. And my neighbors cannot paint their house zebra either. Because if you mess around and paint your house zebra, it is going to bring down our home values. In Tallahassee, for instance, one deed contained a restrictive covenant banning any "noxious or offensive trade" from operating out of that home. If you lived here, you had to know that your dream of owning a pig farm in your backyard would not be possible.

Racially restrictive covenants are a different beast. This same deed in Tallahasee contained the following provision:

> No person of other than the Caucasian race shall own, use or occupy any property in said subdivision except that this covenant shall not prevent occupancy by domestic servants of a different race or nationality employed by an owner or tenant.[22]

In other words, unless you were the help, living in this home as a non-white person would not be possible. Because if you mess around and start letting in Black people, Mexicans, and Asians, *there goes the neighborhood*. Although racially restrictive covenants were ruled unenforceable in 1948, Congress did not outlaw them until the Fair Housing Act of 1968.[23] More than 50 years later, local governments across the country—including Leon County where Tallahassee is located—are trying to address historic racial injustice and have made efforts to remove this language from deeds in county records.[24]

The power of demographics to predict outcomes makes more sense when it becomes clear that until 50 years ago, working hard was not enough to have access to wealth. The Younger family had two choices. They could remain put in a neighborhood where their child playing "catch the rat" is completely normal. Or they could move on up into a neighborhood where they were *just* legally allowed to move into and offered money *not* to move into, knowing that a Black family in a similar situation had their house blown up the day before you were set to move out.

In the ultimate case of adding insult to injury, communities across the country where demographics contributed significantly to the wealth gap are now being displaced because of gentrification. Imagine how it must feel to be geographically bound to a community for generations just to be pushed out? I remember living in the Petworth area of Washington, DC from 2004–2006, pre-gentrification, and seeing strange things starting to happen in the months before I left. One day I came home from school around 7:00 pm and I saw a young white woman jogging through my neighborhood. I turned my head in shock, petrified that this poor woman was lost because she was clearly in the wrong neighborhood. Then a yoga studio opened up across the street from me. And within ten years, I came back to a community where people who had unequal access to wealth were now the majority, and those who were historically deprived of this opportunity were pushed out.

The moral of the then and now case for Tangible Equity is this: we are not dealing with a broken system. Our system is working precisely as it was designed to work. Hundreds of years of intentional actions, laws and policies have gotten us to this unacceptably inequitable place. If we are serious about work needed to reduce the impact of demographics on the predictability of outcomes, we need to be honest about how impactful this work must be. Book studies will not cut it. Doing a privilege walk where students take a step forward or backward depending on the racial, socioeconomic, immigration, parent's income, or other statuses will not do it either.

Tangible Equity obsesses with what this work means at the classroom level because that is the most important unit of change. The scope of the systemic inequities we face as a society is precisely why schools must equip teachers to help students unlock the tools they need to thrive academically, succeed in our current system, and also learn how to lead, innovate, and break the things that must be broken.

Notes

1 Kent, Ana Hernandez. 2021. "Wealth Gaps between White, Black and Hispanic Families in 2019." January 5, 2021. https://www.stlouisfed.org/on-the-economy/2021/january/wealth-gaps-white-black-hispanic-families-2019

2 Blakemore, Erin. 2019. "How the GI Bill's Promise Was Denied to a Million Black WWII Veterans." *HISTORY*. June 27, 2019. https://www.history.com/news/gi-bill-black-wwii-veterans-benefits

3 Heen, Mary L. "Ending Jim Crow Life Insurance Rates." *Northwestern Journal of Law & Social Policy* 4 (2009): 360. http://scholarlycommons.law.northwestern.edu/njlsp/vol4/iss2/3

4 National Geographic Society. 2012. "African American Population." November 9, 2012. https://www.nationalgeographic.org/maps/african-american-population-maps/

5 Sewell, Summer. 2019. "There Were Nearly a Million Black Farmers in 1920. Why Have They Disappeared?" *The Guardian*, April 29, 2019, sec. Environment. https://www.theguardian.com/environment/2019/apr/29/why-have-americas-black-farmers-disappeared

6 Taylor, Steven L. 2013. "The Economics of Slavery." Outside the Beltway. July 20, 2013. https://www.outsidethebeltway.com/the-economics-of-slavery/

7 Packman, Hannah. 2020. "Juneteenth and the Broken Promise of '40 Acres and a Mule.'" National Farmers Union. June 19, 2020. https://nfu.org/2020/06/19/juneteenth-and-the-broken-promise-of-40-acres-and-a-mule/

8 National Agricultural Law Center. 1933. "Agricultural Adjustment Act of 1933." https://nationalaglawcenter.org/wp-content/uploads/assets/farmbills/1933.pdf

9 Lewis, E. E. 1935. "'Black Cotton Farmers and the AAA.'" Teaching American History. https://teachingamericanhistory.org/document/black-cotton-farmers-and-the-aaa/

10 Dovich, Mark, Jeff Chamer, and Hazel Tang. 2021. "USDA Vows to Address 'Historical Discrimination' as Black Farmers Accuse Agency of Racism." *Medill News Service*. September 28, 2021. https://dc.medill.northwestern.edu/blog/2021/09/28/usda-vows-to-address-historical-discrimination-as-black-farmers-accuse-agency-of-racism/#sthash.MGlM6oEP.dpbs

11 Smithsonian Institution Traveling Exhibition Service. n.d. Negro Motorist Green Book. https://negromotoristgreenbook.si.edu/

12 Loewen, James W. 2018. *Sundown Towns: A Hidden Dimension of American Racism*. New York: The New Press.

13 National Archives. 2016. "Records of the Federal Home Loan Bank Board [FHLBB]." August 15, 2016. https://www.archives.gov/research/guide-fed-records/groups/195.html

14 Rothstein, Richard. 2017. *The Color of Law: A Forgotten History of How Our Government Segregated America*. New York; London: Liveright Publishing Corporation, A Division Of W. W. Norton & Company.
15 https://www.amazon.com/Lives-Promise-Valedictorians-Fourteen-year-Achievement/dp/0787901466
16 Nelson, Robert K., LaDale Winling, Richard Marciano, Nathan Connolly, et al., "Mapping Inequality." *American Panorama*, ed. Robert K. Nelson and Edward L. Ayers, accessed October 1, 2021, https://dsl.richmond.edu/panorama/redlining/[YOUR VIEW]
17 Caron, Christina. 2018. "Why Some Italian-Americans Still Fiercely Defend Columbus Day." *The New York Times*. October 5, 2018. https://www.nytimes.com/2018/10/05/us/columbus-day-italians-indigenous-peoples-day.html
18 Hansberry, Lorraine A. (1959) 2007. *A Raisin in the Sun*. Lewes Gmc Distribution. New York, NY: Spark Publishing.
19 The WFMT Studs Terkel Radio Archive. 1959. "Lorraine Hansberry Discusses Her Play 'a Raisin in the Sun.'" May 12, 1959. https://studsterkel.wfmt.com/programs/lorraine-hansberry-discusses-her-play-raisin-sun
20 Wilkerson, Margaret B. "'A Raisin in the Sun': Anniversary of an American Classic." *Theatre Journal* 38, no. 4 (1986): 441–52. https://doi.org/10.2307/3208286
21 Legal Information Institute. 1940. "HANSBERRY et al. v. LEE et al." https://www.law.cornell.edu/supremecourt/text/311/32
22 Waters, TaMaryn. 2019. "Attorney Wants Outdated, Racist Covenant Language in Betton Hills Stripped." Tallahassee Democrat. July 1, 2019. https://www.tallahassee.com/story/news/money/2019/07/01/attorney-wants-outdated-racist-covenant-language-betton-hills-stripped-tallahassee/1546406001/
23 Justice.gov. 2015. "The Fair Housing Act." August 6, 2015. https://www.justice.gov/crt/fair-housing-act-1
24 Silva, Catherine. n.d. "Racial Restrictive Covenants: Enforcing Neighborhood Segregation in Seattle—Seattle Civil Rights and Labor History Project." Accessed October 1, 2021. http://depts.washington.edu/civilr/covenants_report.htm?ncid=edlinkushpmg00000313

Bibliography

Blakemore, Erin. 2019. "How the GI Bill's Promise Was Denied to a Million Black WWII Veterans." *HISTORY*. June 27, 2019. https://www.history.com/news/gi-bill-black-wwii-veterans-benefits

Caron, Christina. 2018. "Why Some Italian-Americans Still Fiercely Defend Columbus Day." *The New York Times*. October 5, 2018. https://www.nytimes.com/2018/10/05/us/columbus-day-italians-indigenous-peoples-day.html

The Commit Partnership. 2021. "Texas Prison Population per Inmate's Last Zip." October 1, 2021. https://commitpartnership.org/dashboard/visualizations/texas-prison-population-per-inmates-last-zip-code

Dovich, Mark, Jeff Chamer, and Hazel Tang. 2021. "USDA Vows to Address 'Historical Discrimination' as Black Farmers Accuse Agency of Racism." *Medill News Service*. September 28, 2021. https://dc.medill.northwestern.edu/blog/2021/09/28/usda-vows-to-address-historical-discrimination-as-black-farmers-accuse-agency-of-racism/#sthash.MGlM6oEP.dpbs

The Food Trust. 2010. "The Grocery Gap: Who Has Access to Healthy Food and Why It Matters." http://thefoodtrust.org/uploads/media_items/grocerygap.original.pdf

Hansberry, Lorraine A. (1959) 2007. *A Raisin in the Sun*. Lewes Gmc Distribution New York, N.Y.: Spark Publishing.

Heen, Mary L. "Ending Jim Crow Life Insurance Rates." *Northwestern Journal of Law & Social Policy* 4 (2009): 360. http://scholarlycommons.law.northwestern.edu/njlsp/vol4/iss2/3

Kent, Ana Hernandez. 2021. "Wealth Gaps between White, Black and Hispanic Families in 2019 St. Louis Fed." January 5, 2021. https://www.stlouisfed.org/on-the-economy/2021/january/wealth-gaps-white-black-hispanic-families-2019

Legal Information Institute. 1940. "HANSBERRY et al. v. LEE et Al." https://www.law.cornell.edu/supremecourt/text/311/32

Lewis, E. E. 1935. "'Black Cotton Farmers and the AAA.'" *Teaching American History*. https://teachingamericanhistory.org/document/black-cotton-farmers-and-the-aaa/

Loewen, James W. 2018. *Sundown Towns: A Hidden Dimension of American Racism*. New York: The New Press.

Lorraine Hansberry Discusses Her Play 'a Raisin in the Sun'. 1959. *The WFMT Studs Terkel Radio Archive*. May 12, 1959. https://studsterkel.wfmt.com/programs/lorraine-hansberry-discusses-her-play-raisin-sun

National Agricultural Law Center. 1933. "Agricultural Adjustment Act of 1933." https://nationalaglawcenter.org/wp-content/uploads/assets/farmbills/1933.pdf

National Archives. 2016. "Records of the Federal Home Loan Bank Board [FHLBB]." August 15, 2016. https://www.archives.gov/research/guide-fed-records/groups/195.html

National Geographic Society. 2012. "African American Population." November 9, 2012. https://www.nationalgeographic.org/maps/african-american-population-maps/

Nelson, Robert K., LaDale Winling, Richard Marciano, Nathan Connolly, et al., "Mapping Inequality." In *American Panorama*, edited by Robert K. Nelson and Edward L. Ayers, accessed October 1, 2021, https://dsl.richmond.edu/panorama/redlining/[YOUR VIEW]

Packman, Hannah. 2020. "Juneteenth and the Broken Promise of '40 Acres and a Mule'." *National Farmers Union*. June 19, 2020. https://nfu.org/2020/06/19/juneteenth-and-the-broken-promise-of-40-acres-and-a-mule/

Rothstein, Richard. 2017. *The Color of Law: A Forgotten History of How Our Government Segregated America*. New York; London: Liveright Publishing Corporation, A Division Of W. W. Norton & Company.

Sewell, Summer. 2019. "There Were Nearly a Million Black Farmers in 1920. Why Have They Disappeared?" *The Guardian*. April 29, 2019, sec. Environment. https://www.theguardian.com/environment/2019/apr/29/why-have-americas-black-farmers-disappeared

Silva, Catherine. n.d. "Racial Restrictive Covenants: Enforcing Neighborhood Segregation in Seattle—Seattle Civil Rights and Labor History Project." Accessed October 1, 2021. http://depts.washington.edu/civilr/covenants_report.htm?ncid=edlinkushpmg00000313

Smithsonian Institution Traveling Exhibition Service. n.d. *Negro Motorist Green Book*. https://negromotoristgreenbook.si.edu/

Taylor, Steven L. 2013. "The Economics of Slavery." Outside the Beltway. July 20, 2013. https://www.outsidethebeltway.com/the-economics-of-slavery/

Waters, TaMaryn. 2019. "Attorney Wants Outdated, Racist Covenant Language in Betton Hills Stripped." *Tallahassee Democrat*. July 1, 2019. https://www.tallahassee.com/story/news/money/2019/07/01/attorney-wants-outdated-racist-covenant-language-betton-hills-stripped-tallahassee/1546406001/

Wilkerson, Margaret B. "'A Raisin in the Sun': Anniversary of an American Classic." *Theatre Journal* 38, no. 4 (1986): 441–52. https://doi.org/10.2307/3208286

4

Avoiding Extreme Optimism and Extreme Pessimism

Doom and gloom is not really my style. After reading the last chapter's deep dive into the deep, systemic inequities that play a significant role in inequities that still exist today, you may disagree. But it is so important that as we approach this work, we avoid the kind of extreme optimism or extreme pessimism that stifles momentum and incentives inaction.

Racism did not end when the Civil Rights Act was signed or when President Obama won his election. But this does not mean we cannot acknowledge the giant leaps we have made as a society when it comes to racial relations and increasing opportunity for all. I do not condone violence, but I understand the urge to throat-punch any edu-celebrity who says "education hasn't changed in 100 years." 100 years ago I could not go to school with white children, period. We, almost universally, refused to teach children in languages other than English. Yes, schools, like neighborhoods, are still more segregated than the *Brown v. Board of Education* court would have anticipated 60 years later. Yes, our work with English Language Learners leaves a lot to be desired. But I would be doing this Tangible Equity work a great disservice

DOI: 10.4324/9781003282464-6

if we did not acknowledge that the revolutionary history of the work we stand upon allows us to see the hope for drastic change.

In 2016, I had the honor of delivering a keynote address at a casino on the Las Vegas Strip as part of an annual Dr Martin Luther King Jr Scholarship Gala. I remember taking the time for a visual picture of what it looked like standing at the podium in this fancy casino convention center. It gave me hope to recognize these amazing people in this amazing room full of amazingly accomplished Black folks including Black elected officials, C-level executives, lawyers, doctors, and business owners. It gave me hope because I recognized that no level of amazing would have allowed these people to convene on the Las Vegas Strip 50 years ago.

I was also honored because I was, and still am, able to stand on stages with the formal title of Colin Seale, Esq., licensed Nevada attorney. After a wild experience of teaching by day, going to law school by night, graduating at the top of my class, and scoring a high-paying job at the most prestigious law firm in Las Vegas, I passed the bar and started practicing law. But the honor was not because of my achievements. The honor came from my knowledge of what me practicing law represented.

I am a child of immigrants from Barbados who moved from the East Coast to Las Vegas. In the early 1960s, Charles Kellar, an experienced Black attorney with the NAACP was more accomplished than I could imagine tried to do the same thing. He came from the East Coast. He was actually born in Barbados just like my family was. But we had a lot of differences. When I took the bar, I got a hotel room next to the testing center and someone from my fancy law firm bought me lunch each day. But when Kellar came to Reno, NV to take the bar exam, he slept two nights in the Reno airport because no hotel would take him in. When I took the bar, I left about an hour early each day. And because I used rappers like Jay-Z, Nas, and Biggie in all of my hypothetical scenarios in my essays, I recognized later that three model essay responses for that year's bar exams were mine. Kellar was the first Black attorney to pass the Nevada State Bar exam, but because his score was too high, he was accused of cheating and failed Nevada's character exam for attorneys. He was already an attorney authorized to practice law in multiple states! He did everything he was supposed to do. But he still had to wait five years for the Nevada Supreme Court to let him in.[1]

The balance I urge you to strike is guided by a question Dr King posed in his 1966 speech: "Are we really making any progress in race relations?"[2] For context, this was right after the passage of the Civil Rights Act of 1964 and the Voters Right Act of 1965, and Dr King pointed out that some folks, "the extreme optimists," would point to these great legislative accomplishments and pronounce "problem solved!" But there was another set of people: the "extreme pessimists," who believed that we were creating more problems than we solved: the Ku Klux Klan's violent tactics were at an all-time high, cities were burning because of racial strife, and these extreme pessimists believed that fundamentally, there could be no real progress in racial relations.

Dr King concluded that both the extreme optimist and the extreme pessimist share one fatal characteristic: the desire to stop fighting against racial injustice. The extreme optimist figures that if everything is cupcakes and rainbows, we ought to simply rejoice and be glad about how far we have come. From this perspective, Summer 2020's global mass protests against racial injustice in the United States were completely uncalled for. Dr Martin Luther King, Jr has a national holiday and a massive monument at the National Mall. In the 1920s, only 10,000—one out of every 1000—Black people had a college degree. Today, 20% of Blacks over 25 have at least a college degree. A million more have master's degrees and 300,000 more have doctorates or degrees in law, business, and medicine. There is no need to work towards racial justice because that work has already been done, successfully.

I lived the experience of becoming the extreme pessimist, who is equally likely to become stagnant in this work. Weeks after the September 11, 2001 attacks that hit our large base of New York City students hard at Syracuse University, I decided to run for Student Body President. On my 19th birthday a couple of months later, I won the election. But I faced an immediate crisis of conscience when the university announced Mayor Rudolph Giuliani—then dubbed "America's mayor"—as the

Commencement Speaker. Giuliani was Time Magazine's Man of the Year in 2001[3] and the "majority" of students at Syracuse University, a predominately white institution, were thrilled by his invitation.

The problem was, over 80% of Syracuse University's Black and Latinx population came from New York City. Giuliani's presence at a unifying, celebratory event like a college graduation ceremony meant something different to us. It reminded us that Giuliani's record of cleaning up the streets and being tough on crime, meant that the humiliating and dehumanizing stop-and-frisk program was a part of the daily experience of young people of color in New York City.[4] It brought back painful memories of Amadou Diallo, an unarmed, African immigrant being shot 41 times for pulling out his wallet to show his ID per officer request.[5] And it reminded me of being 16 years old, being around the corner from my home in Brooklyn, NY, and having police officers stop and frisk me.

I was one of few Black students attending the prestigious Bronx High School of Science and I was getting ready to start a week-long mechanical engineering summer program at Manhattan College the next day. But none of that mattered when the sirens rang. I was pushed up against a brick wall being searched and aggressively questioned about where I was coming from and where I was going. It might not sound like much to be questioned about where you are coming from and where you are going. But I was raised to understand that this was the land of the free. Yet, I still had to very respectfully justify my movements to angry men as the only way out of the shamefully deadly crime of walking while Black. This moment permanently stripped me of my full humanity. This idea of America, this promise that lit up my family's eyes in the depths of their dark struggle to immigrate to the United States was betrayed. This firm belief that their American children will be entitled to life, liberty, and the pursuit of happiness, and that all will be well if you just do the right thing, was shattered.

But I was Student Body President, and over 500 students signed a petition asking me to do something about this. This wasn't an event sponsored by the College Republicans or a special Speakers' Series. This was commencement, where every student was being invited to hear a keynote address from an extremely divisive figure. I had to do something. I had to say something. This was not okay. And I was only 19 years old, but I was in a position of power to say this was not okay.

And when I did this, I had a momentary sense of optimism. Of hope. Because somehow I urged the Student Association to pass a bill officially denouncing Giuliani's invitation, and the bill passed. But I was not ready for what followed. The paper the next day had an opinion piece written by two white students that started with "Colin Seale, you are a joke" and continued to explain that they always knew I was an idiot, but they "obviously underestimated my stupidity." I stayed in my office for hours, responding to emails from Syracuse University alumni trashing me. I was 19 years old. One of those emails informed me that I was "the reason racial profiling exists." Another one said "Colin Seale…memorizing that name…never, ever, hiring this idiot."

I spent that semester digging myself into a hole. Reading every single negative email written to me. Somehow I ended up on Fox News on Greta Van Sustren's show, not realizing the ridicule I was going to endure on a primetime show. I kindly declined to appear on The O'Reilly Factor the next day. But I did read national op-eds talking about how stupid I was. I was 19 years old. I had to withdraw from my morning classes because I couldn't bring myself to wake up in the mornings. I almost lost my scholarships because of how much time I spent replying to racist alumni emails like the ones reminding me that "I was the reason racial profiling existed.". And worst yet, I became the extreme pessimist.

What was the point of speaking up against injustice, if when you do, you just get your spirit crushed. Giuliani still spoke,[6] some students stood up and turned their backs at him while holding up their wallets in honor of Amadou Diallo, but he still spoke. A couple of weeks later, a white fraternity had a golf shirt party, and one student decided to paint his face Black so he could be Tiger Woods. I felt like an organized effort to speak up against an action that negatively impacted

Black students became a rallying cry for racists to come out of hiding—and this is in a school serving the most liberal corridor of our nation. So, what was the point?

Fortunately, Dr King acknowledged a third type of outlook on racial relations: not the extreme optimist, not the extreme pessimist, but the realist. The realist in race relations trying to answer the question of progress would seek to combine the trues of two opposites, while avoiding the extremes of both. And so, the realist would agree with the optimist that we have come a long, long way, but he would seek to balance that by agreeing with the pessimist in that we have a long, long way to go.

Tangible Equity must be approached with this balanced, realist approach to change. Dr King gave us additional guidance on how to do this in an essay he prepared as a college student writing about the purpose of education: "Education must enable one to sift and weigh evidence, to discern the true from the false, the real from the unreal, and the facts from the fiction." He added that intelligence is not enough--Intelligence plus character--that is the goal of true education. The complete education gives one not only power of concentration, but worthy objectives upon which to concentrate."[7]

Going forward, I challenge you to concentrate on worthy objectives and move beyond mere optimism with no action or pessimism with no action. Instead, embrace the realist approach to advancing this work in your classroom and beyond. Because although we have come a long, long way, we still have a long, long way to go and for that reason, the work must continue.

Notes

1 White, Claytee, Geralda Miller, and Charles Kellar. 1909. "Challenging Expectations CHARLES L. KELLAR: Legal Trailblazer in Nevada." https://www.nvbar.org/wp-content/uploads/NevLawyer_2012_Kellar-1.pdf
2 King, Martin Luther, Jr. 2015. "Transcript of Dr Martin Luther King's Speech at SMU on March 17, 1966—SMU." https://www.smu.edu/News/2014/mlk-at-smu-transcript-17march1966

3 Pooley, Eric. 2001. "Mayor of the World." *Time*. December 31, 2001. http://content.time.com/time/specials/packages/article/0,28804,2020227_2020306,00.html
4 Bridge Initiative Team. 2020. "Factsheet: NYPD STOP and FRISK POLICY." Bridge Initiative. June 5, 2020. https://bridge.georgetown.edu/research/factsheet-nypd-stop-and-frisk-policy/
5 Red, Christian. 2019. "Years before Black Lives Matter, 41 Shots Killed Him." *The New York Times*. July 19, 2019. https://www.nytimes.com/2019/07/19/nyregion/amadou-diallo-mother-eric-garner.html
6 Syracuse University News. 2002. "Commencement Address by Rudolph Giuliani—Syracuse University News." May 21, 2002. https://news.syr.edu/blog/2002/05/21/commencement-address-by-rudolph-giuliani/
7 King, Jr. Martin Luther. 2017. "'The Purpose of Education'." The Martin Luther King, Jr, Research and Education Institute. May 3, 2017. https://kinginstitute.stanford.edu/king-papers/documents/purpose-education

Bibliography

Bridge Initiative Team. 2020. "Factsheet: NYPD STOP and FRISK POLICY." Bridge Initiative. June 5, 2020. https://bridge.georgetown.edu/research/factsheet-nypd-stop-and-frisk-policy/

King, Martin Luther, Jr. 2015. "Transcript of Dr Martin Luther King's Speech at SMU on March 17, 1966—SMU." https://www.smu.edu/News/2014/mlk-at-smu-transcript-17march1966

King, Martin Luther, Jr. 2017. "'The Purpose of Education'." The Martin Luther King, Jr, Research and Education Institute. May 3, 2017. https://kinginstitute.stanford.edu/king-papers/documents/purpose-education

Pooley, Eric. 2001. "Mayor of the World." *Time*. December 31, 2001. http://content.time.com/time/specials/packages/article/0,28804,2020227_2020306,00.html

Red, Christian. 2019. "Years before Black Lives Matter, 41 Shots Killed Him." *The New York Times*. July 19, 2019. https://www.nytimes.com/2019/07/19/nyregion/amadou-diallo-mother-eric-garner.html

Syracuse University News. 2002. "Commencement Address by Rudolph Giuliani—Syracuse University News." May 21, 2002. https://news.syr.edu/blog/2002/05/21/commencement-address-by-rudolph-giuliani/

White, Claytee, Geralda Miller, and Charles Kellar. 1909. "Challenging Expectations CHARLES L. KELLAR: Legal Trailblazer in Nevada." https://www.nvbar.org/wp-content/uploads/NevLawyer_2012_Kellar-1.pdf

Part II

The “How” of Tangible Equity

5

Beyond Good People with Good Intentions

The pursuit of Tangible Equity is a deeply personal journey, a journey I believed I was uniquely qualified to undertake as a first-year teacher. My decision to teach math in Washington, DC after graduating with my Computer Science degree at Syracuse University was a no-brainer for at least three reasons. First, I started my own math tutoring business at 12 years old because although I was on free and reduced lunch, my tastebuds were way too refined to eat the gray cheeseburgers served in the Intermediate School 285 cafeteria. Also, I knew I had a "way" of helping struggling math students in my East Flatbush neighborhood connect with math content. So, while other kids in my Brooklyn, NY neighborhood were becoming exposed to potentially addictive drugs and alcohol, I was already over-exposed to the undeniably addictive thrill of watching kids my age and younger experience those lightbulb, a-ha moments.

My experience teaching math and the joy I got from seeing students "get it" were nothing compared to my final reason for teaching math: I just had to. As a child of immigrants raised in a single parent home with a father incarcerated for a decade for selling drugs, I admit that this sense of responsibility did not

DOI: 10.4324/9781003282464-8

make a whole lot of sense to my mother. Especially since my decision to teach meant that I would be deferring my admission to Syracuse University's Maxwell School of Public Citizenship and Public Affairs' Master's in Public Administration program, the top-ranked MPA program in the country to this day.[1] Teaching meant I wasn't just deferring admission, I was also risking the full-ride scholarship I received to complete this program. And it was not just tuition! As a Ronald E. McNair graduate fellow, I was also risking a $20,000 stipend I was set to receive with the sole condition that I could not work while completing this rigorous one-year program. Why? Because I just had to.

I did not have my first Black male teacher until sixth grade, Mr Joseph. Mr Joseph was not actually my teacher, he was my coach. If you are thinking he was my basketball or football coach, you are wrong (and I will talk later about how our *explicit* bias plays a huge role in making these type of assumptions), because Mr Joseph was actually my math team coach. He and my amazing math teacher Ms Williams took this energetic, loud, obnoxious group of South Brooklyn kids from three different elementary school self-contained gifted programs and lit us on fire. With their support and advocacy, we became the first class in our district to take the equivalent of Algebra I in seventh grade. If Mr Joseph was amazing, Mr McNeil, the Black male math teacher I had in seventh and eighth grade was a walking inspiration. His humor, his contagious energy, and his "dollar" problems (which I'm still salty he never let me try because he used them to get our quieter students to come up to the board) inspired me to start teaching math as a seventh grader.

So when I had the chance to be the same kind of role model to young Black boys in Washington, DC, I simply had no choice. The unique privilege to be a role model like Mr Joseph and Mr McNeil were to me made teaching my why, my mission, and my purpose. In 2004, in pre-gentrification Washington, DC when you could still legitimately call this place "Chocolate City," I ended up being the only Black male educator on my team. Being a role model to young Black boys felt like an even bigger part of my why, my mission, and my purpose given these circumstances. It would be amazing if I could tell you that the power behind my mission, my shared background of growing up with similar struggles as these boys, and my shared identity with these boys led them to transformational, positive outcomes. Unfortunately, I cannot tell you that story. That story does not exist. The story that does exist is a humiliating one.

The real story is that by the end of the first semester, I was referring twice as many Black boys out of class than anyone else on my team. I was the only Black male educator. Being a positive role model to Black boys was my why, my mission, and my purpose. And I was *still* kicking Black boys out of class at twice the rate as anyone else on my team, putting them on the bullet train through the school-to-prison pipeline. How does that make any sense? Some might argue that I had higher expectations for them, holding them up to a higher standard. If that was legit, then why would I be so quick to ensure their academic demise by taking them out of classes? Being such a huge part of why some of them were kicked out of school altogether?

It turns out that I demonstrated *explicit* bias towards my Black boys. This explicit bias was not about the quantitative data showing that I wrote my Black boys up at twice the rate of anyone else on my team. It was also qualitative. Qualitatively, I felt the explicit bias in its rawest forms and remember these feelings as if they are happening as I am writing this sentence. I can tell you with 100% certainty that when a Black boy in my class engaged in the common middle school behavior of throwing a balled-up piece of paper at another student, I felt my blood boiling at such an extreme rate, even though I would shrug my shoulders if any other child were to do the same.

This was not about high expectations or a higher standard. This was about the fears that stuck with me as the kid who went to the nerdy high school, spent the summer before my senior year in an engineering program, and still got pushed against the wall and stopped-and-frisked by police for walking while Black. This was about three out the 24 students who were in my self-contained gifted class in elementary school getting kicked out of high school (all Black boys). My explicit bias against Black boys came from my full understanding that the world was going to be unfairly harsh to them so I had to prepare them for this harshness with tough love. It breaks my heart to recognize how wrong this was, especially since I was uniquely qualified to show them *love* love. It is humiliating and painful to come to terms with the reality that my actions based on my explicit bias caused real harm to my students.

But there is an important Tangible Equity lesson to be learned here. My good intentions; the fact that being a role model to Black boys was my why, my mission, and my purpose did not protect me from perpetuating systemic inequities. My shared background of growing up in the struggle did not protect me perpetuating systemic inequities. My shared identity as a Black male did not protect me from perpetuating systemic inequities. The only way I could meaningfully and intentionally work to reverse my problematic practices was engage in the four-step process I refer to as the RACK Framework for Restoring the Harm of Explicit Bias, shown in Figure 5.1:

This RACK process recognizes that our good intentions are not good enough when our actual actions cause harm. I need to name that explicit bias does not necessarily refer to bias based on race, ethnicity, sexual orientation, gender identity, or immigration status. We can cause harm to students when we are explicitly biased towards students who share the interests we loved as children and against students who shared interests we hated.

R	**Reflect** honestly on my explicit bias without judgement and with a clear understanding that in some way, in some form, my explicit bias is doing harm to students.
A	**Acknowledge** (a) the harm your explicit bias is causing and (b) the concrete actions you engage in that lead to this harm.
C	**Change** your actions to counteractions that stop this harm and restore our students.
K	**Keep** reflecting, acknowledging, changing, and spreading the word, recognizing that we all have some level of explicit bias within us that, left unchecked, can lead to harm to students.

FIGURE 5.1
RACK Framework for Restoring the Harm of Explicit Bias.

If I had a theater student who had to leave my class early to prep for a school musical, the theater guy in me was over the moon! "Break a leg! I can't wait to see you later!" Meanwhile, if I had a student who needed to leave early to get to his football game, I could easily find myself thinking, "Okay, future NFL prospect. Enjoy the game, I guess. I hope you really break a leg!" Honestly I never said that, but I think we need to get more comfortable being uncomfortable with the hard truths around explicit bias. Still don't believe explicit bias is ubiquitous in our work? Try teaching a child with personality traits and behaviors that remind you of a child who bullied you growing up. Think about the explicit bias of teachers who struggle to name their own children because certain names bring up students whom they would never want to conjure up when saying their own child's name.

Knowing when to apply the RACK Framework for Preventing Explicit Bias Harm can be challenging. I can advise you to use this whenever you say something, think something, or hear something that raises eyebrows, but this is not useful. It is easy to become so normalized around inequity that you fail to notice anything is wrong. In other words, there are no magic glasses to help you to view education with an equity lens.

Functionally, this means you should apply this lens any and every time you make a significant decision or feel a significant emotion (anger, sympathy, frustration, happiness, laughter). Doing this correctly requires a presumption that nothing is 100% neutral. For example, the concept of data-driven instruction is relatively non-controversial. The idea of using data on student academic performance to guide instructional decisions is a bedrock principle of modern education. So why does RACK apply? Because you make a significant decision when you decide how you interpret data and how you will teach students based on your interpretation. Data-driven instruction is not all that non-controversial when you RACK it up:

1. **Reflect** honestly on your explicit bias without judgment and with a clear understanding that in some way, in some form, your explicit bias is doing harm to students.

Reflecting often takes the form of a stream-of-consciousness conversation focusing on all the ways this significant decision or emotion may trigger my explicit biases. In this case, data-driven instruction involves a lot of subjective decision-making. It is easy to reduce my students to a number instead of the full human beings they are. There is a tremendous bias towards quantitative data that ignores the important qualitative data that can give me better context. Every year I taught eighth grade, for instance, students scored miserably on beginning-of-year diagnostics. I also noticed that this same group of students forgot how to open their lockers even though they did so hundreds of times in the last two years. If my data probe leads me to an understanding that my students are "too low" to engage in rigorous, grade-level content, my data-driven decisions may result in an all-too-common lowering of the bar that ensures my struggling learners stay "low." Considering the perfectionist tendencies and deficit orientations educators commonly share, data dives so often shift our priorities towards student weaknesses and what they do not know instead of their strengths and what they do know.

2. **Acknowledge** (a) the harm your explicit bias is causing and (b) the concrete actions you engage in that lead to this harm.

After you engage in the reflection process where you list all of the ways your significant decision or significant feeling *may* trigger your explicit bias, think through the most important way it actually *does* trigger your explicit bias. In my first year of teaching in Washington, DC, my practice of treating students like data points did tremendous damage. My fear of "low" students falling behind forced me to teach the simplest, least-rigorous version of everything the whole class. I would lash out with anger if one of my "low" students misbehaved, was off-task, or if one of my "high" students distracted one my "low" students. I felt like a clown when I learned that several of my "low" students were actually not "low" at all. They just rose to the level of my low expectations and stayed there. Even worse, my "high" students gradually lost interest because my data-driven decision was the starting pistol for the race to the bottom.

3. **Change** your actions to counteractions that stop this harm and restore our students.

This will be discussed more in the next chapter, but for now, recognize that this is a special type of change. Here, change means you are not just stopping the harmful conduct, but working intentionally to reverse it. I should warn you that this is a space where the counterintuitive often prevails against the intuitive. For instance, the best way to stop the harm and restore students harmed by the explicit bias in my data-driven instruction was to teach my whole class, including the "low" students, in a way that challenged my "high" students tremendously. This sounds ridiculous on its face, but as you will see in Chapter 10, Teaching to the Top shifted my expectations in students and students' expectations in themselves in a way that transformed achievement. To make these changes stick, I go through the Six P's for addressing educational inequities in the next chapter.

4. **Keep** reflecting, acknowledging, changing, and spreading the word recognizing that we all have some level of explicit bias within us that, left unchecked, can lead to harm to students.

It goes without saying, but once you realize that data-driven instruction is ripe for decisions grounded in explicit bias, you cannot un-realize that. Every piece of data from parent surveys, attendance records, standardized exams and even informal thumbs-up/thumbs-down formative assessment data lends itself to a RACK process whenever it involves a significant decision or feeling. For systemic change, you have to be able to spread the word, speak out, and push your colleagues on this. If you, for instance, are in a critical thinking training with a colleague who analyzes the test scores of his roster and concludes "these kids can't," that is a RACK moment. Tracking students in classes, assigning students to academic intervention courses, and dividing students into ability-based groups are also RACK moments. Deciding which students get awards and which ones do not are incredibly important RACK moments. I'm sure no teacher kept careful quantitative records on how much I got on their nerves, but no amount of academic achievement could enable me to be selected as Student of the Month at any point of my K-12 experience.

Tangible Equity is not about being a good person. It is not about having good intentions. It is about understanding that we are human beings with explicit biases that inform our decisions and our emotions. And as I will discuss in the next chapter, our decisions and our emotions have tremendous power.

Note

1 US News and World Report. 2021. "Best Public Affairs Programs: Ranked in 2021." https://www.usnews.com/best-graduate-schools/top-public-affairs-schools/public-affairs-rankings

6

The Six P's for Actually Doing Something about Educational Inequities

In the last chapter, I discussed how educators can benefit from the RACK process (**R**eflect, **A**cknowledge, **C**hange, and **K**eep reflecting, acknowledging and changing) to increase awareness of inequities. The hardest step of the RACK process is the *change* piece, because change is hard enough by itself. Change is even harder because of what I like to call the Paper Straw Problem. Even the most hardcore environmentalist has to admit that drinking out of paper straws is not much fun. If you are like me and are used to biting plastic straws, you now must get used to actually eating paper straws. Even non-biters get annoyed at paper straws for turning to mush if you do not inhale your drink in two minutes or less. But the Paper Straw Problem is a lot bigger than this.

Despite the frustrations of paper straws, it is probably a solid choice if I want to protect the environment. But am I really protecting the environment? I, and a million other people, can drink paper straws every day for the next hundred years and not come close to matching the carbon footprint of fossil fuel

DOI: 10.4324/9781003282464-9

emissions. Nothing about this paper straw can undo all the toxins certain factories put into the air we breathe or the toxic waste certain businesses pour into the water we drink.

The Paper Straw Problem speaks to one of the most common reasons educators have struggled to make equity real at the classroom level: the system seems so stacked against this effort. Tangible Equity seems compelling in theory. But when it comes to the practicalities involved in trying to reduce the predictive power of demographics as a classroom teacher, thousands of educators have told me some version of this hopeless admission: "I am just a teacher."

Just a teacher, to me, is an outrageous statement. Teachers are inherently powerful. A particular young man's journey through our education system is the most compelling example I can think of that explains the power of educators. The young man in question is Christopher Wallace, also known as The Notorious BIG, also known as Biggie Smalls. Biggie is one of the greatest rappers of all time and I always loved him because his story feels a lot like my story. He is the child of Caribbean immigrants, just like me. He grew up in a single parent household just like me. He is also from Brooklyn, he also grew up in the struggle, and he had a hard time in high school. And Biggie, like three of the brilliant students I went to elementary school with, did not finish high school.

Our paths change at the point where Biggie starts dealing drugs and gets locked up for doing so. But he is so talented and gifted as a rapper that he ends of getting signed on Bad Boy Records, the hottest new record label founded by up-and-coming producer Sean "Puffy" Combs (before he was Puff Daddy, P Diddy, Diddy, or whatever he is calling himself at the time you end up reading this book). Biggie knew his first album *Ready to Die*[1] was going to be huge hit because his first single, *Juicy*, was an instant classic. This was his "momma we made it" moment. So, when Biggie is going back and doing the ad-libs for the first single on his first album, to whom does Biggie dedicate his album?

To his teachers! And as I am sharing this, maybe some of you who are not as familiar with Biggie's music must be thinking of how amazingly thoughtful that was of him. Maybe you are thinking about those teachers you had who believed in you even when you did not believe in yourself. Those educators who pushed you even when you were flat out unlikeable. The teachers who never leave our minds because they have never left our hearts. But in Biggie's case, the teachers who never left his mind and never left his heart did not fit this profile.

"Yeah, this album is dedicated to all the teachers that told me I'd never amount to nothin."[2] At the moment that Biggie has fulfilled the promise of the American dream that his family dreamed about when they immigrated from Jamaica, his "momma we made it" moment, the pinnacle of success, he chose to dedicate his first words on his first single on his first album to the teachers who did not believe in him.

Tangible Equity requires that phrases like "just a teacher" must be retired. There is no such thing as "just a teacher." Teachers have the power to unlock magic. Teachers also have the power to crush young souls. Teachers have the power to hold a mirror up students so they can see their own power. Teachers have the power to create a child's lifelong sense of doubt and they have the power to create a child's lifelong sense of self-confidence.

Power is the first of Six P's that can support your efforts to change inequitable practices or policies as part of the RACK process. In the upcoming chapters, these will be broken down in detail to give you a powerful, but practical guide to make equity real at the classroom, school, or system level as shown in Figure 6.1

Power

Power is the first of the "Six P's for *Actually* Doing Something About Educational Inequities". You do not have the sole power to change your state's graduation requirements or to end the inequitable practice of funding schools based on local property tax bases. But I can name several areas where I had unequivocable power as a classroom teacher; decisions where I never had to check in with an administrator or get anyone's approval.

Power	What are two-three areas you have decision-making authority over?
Priorities	What is one area you can focus on as priority for fighting racial inequalities?
Probe	What information, data, and/or resources do you need?
Privilege	How, specifically, can you leverage your privilege to make this change happen?
People	Who do you need to make this happen?
Problems	What roadblocks, pushback, and challenges can you anticipate and plan to overcome?

FIGURE 6.1
The Six P's for *Actually* Doing Something about Educational Inequities.

I had the power to ask my students how they were doing and actually care about the answer. I had the power to set expectations, to welcome student voice, to choose the attitude I showed up with, and to decide whether this was my classroom or a space where students felt a sense of ownership over their classroom.

Before you can do something about the educational inequities we witness through the RACK process discussed in the previous chapter, you must name and understand your power. Power is not a comfortable word, especially for those of us used to having power used against us. But power, by itself, is a neutral concept. Power can come from our positional power, as we see in teacher-student, parent-child, principal-teacher relationships. Power can also come from organized money or organized people as we often see in political and community organizing movements. But the power I am referring to is the power you have to act within the scope of your authority.

Educators who engage in equity work without reflection often develop a troubling superpower: the ability to spot all the inequities in the world without being able to see the inequities that are right in front of them. For example, I have a white colleague who is an amazing professor of education at a prestigious university who cares deeply about fighting for racial justice. During a protest against racial injustice in her community, the operator of a popular franchise location began berating the diverse crowd of protesters, threatening them, and using racial slurs. Because I am still a licensed attorney, she reached out to see if there was anything that could be done to reach out to the national franchise owner about shutting down or disciplining this franchise. I had worked on a case involving franchise law before, so I shared some of what I knew and some of the potential complications. It meant a lot to me that she cared so much about this issue.

She was taken aback, however, when I started to ask her about injustices that were a lot closer to her. How many tenured Black faculty are in your department? How many Black faculty, period, are in your department? How many Black Ph.D. students are in your department's programs? For students of color in your Ph.D. programs, do you notice any patterns around their levels of success in the program? Of course, you have every right to be outraged about the conduct of this franchise operator. But right now, as an influential scholar, you have the power to speak up on injustices in your own department. Of course, you have every right to research the ins and outs of franchise law to see how you can hold this franchise operator accountable. But you have the actual power to research the ins and outs of the role that demographics play in the predictability of outcomes for your hiring processes, student selection processes, and student success in your undergraduate and graduate programs.

In organizing work, power maps are typically used to help advocates visualize whom they need to rally, influence, or leverage to create a desired outcome. In Tangible Equity work, the only person on the power map is you. As a bus driver, you have the power to memorize the names of every child you pick up so you can greet each by name each morning. As a school principal, you have the power to be a visible presence in your teachers' classrooms so teachers and students see you and understand that you care about *seeing* and care to be *seen*. As an educator with power, YOU are the latitude, longitude, legend, and sole destination on your personal power map.

Priorities

Prioritization is one of the hardest parts of teaching. Determining what matters, when, and to what extent requires a constant juggling act even when no glaring inequities exist. But when inequities run rampant, figuring out where to start is overwhelming. The cliché question-answer adage of "How do you eat an elephant? One bite at a time." has no practical purpose for the overwhelmed educator who cannot sit around munching on elephants for all of eternity.

I felt the "where do I start" challenge deeply when I started teaching in Washington, DC. In the same school year, I had a student who showed up two or three times a month because her apartment building's poor ventilation caused wild flare-ups with her asthma. A student's HIV-positive mother passed away. One of my star ninth-grade mathletes was impregnated through a gang rape and miscarried a few months later. Students who needed glasses did not have access to glasses in a city with no fewer than five community non-profits designed to solve this problem. In the midst of all the challenges my students faced outside of school, my school had draconian disciplinary practices. Once students reached a certain number of bad behavior points, they could end up out of class for months through our in-school suspension program. I struggled with this policy, even though my explicit bias towards Black boys played an important part in pushing them into in-school suspension.

While the disparate in-school suspension practices were the most negatively impactful to students, one particular practice truly made me question why I was in education. I was a kid who got so much life from the clear stamp of approval that came from a rowdy, boisterous audience of Brooklyn students enjoying a performance or celebrating a friend winning an award by shouting, screaming out their names, or even standing on their chairs in approval of a job well done. At the first assembly of the year, a sixth grader's good friend received an award. Like any good friend would do, she stood up and starting screaming her friend's name. From the stage, the administrator with the microphone pointed at this excited girl and told her to exit, immediately. Because at this school, we do "respectful" applause. Apparently, school uniforms and draconian disciplinary policies were not controlling enough. This school also believed in controlling joy.

It would have been so easy for me to become a hopeless pessimist who felt like action was futile. It is easy to understand how any educator faced with similar levels and frequencies of injustice can end up feeling the same way. And to be clear, while all of my teaching experience occurred in economically disadvantaged communities serving almost entirely Black and Latinx student populations, unbearable inequities exist everywhere. Analyzing education with a RACK framework is like taking the red pill in *The Matrix*; you will likely find serious inequities in almost every major policy, practice, and decision that impacts children. The Tangible Equity process of prioritization helps you focus your efforts by focusing on the first P: power.

To prioritize your efforts against educational inequities, start with the issues that align most closely to the areas you have the most power over. This chapter is about *actually* doing something about inequities. Our students' out-of-school challenges are definitely important. But classroom educators do not have direct power over solving those out-of-school issues. Classroom educators are also not the cause of those out-of-school issues. This is not saying that you ignore issues outside of your scope of power. Teachers are mandated reporters and resource connectors who are often the first to know that a child is in need. But, most of that *actual* work is done by a third party. If you want to prioritize *your* work, you should start with *your* power.

You always have the power to advocate and speak out against unjust policies and practices at the school level. I believe this is actually how we are wired. Young children make federal cases about bedtime and eating vegetables. Teenagers scream "that's not fair" about dress codes and curfews. Remember earlier when I noted that our negative relationship with power comes from the common experience of how power has often been used against us? The corollary to that point is that we are so used to prioritizing issues that involve the fight *against* other people's power that we avoid prioritizing the issues that involve the fight that *aligns* to our own power.

Tactically, prioritizing within the scope of your own power also makes a lot of practical sense. I do not know what sort of credibility I would carry if I railed against the school's draconian disciplinary practices at a time when I was the worst offender of exacerbating these problems in my classroom. On the other hand, imagine the impact of prioritizing my problematic practice of kicking Black boys out of class at twice the rate of other teachers. Whatever reality resulted from that change can now serve as an exemplar I can point to, allowing my individual change to transform to a systemic one.

Keeping your scope of power in mind, what is the most obvious area for you to address inequities in your policies and practices—both the written and the unwritten ones? When you analyze inequities in academic data, attendance data, parent engagement data, student participation data, and disciplinary data, what particular inequity has the dual quality of 1) lighting a fire under you because of how frustrating, painful, unfair, or unacceptable it is and 2) being closely aligned with your personal power map?

Educators engaged in this work with me over the last few years have done a great job of choosing priorities. The hiring manager for one school system prioritized diversifying the teacher candidate pool and diversifying talent pipelines for promotional opportunities because she could not shake the vastly different racial makeup between her students and her teachers. The hiring manager had unequivocal power over setting up policies, practices, and systems to make this change possible.

A teacher prioritized "leaving curriculum alone" because he recognized that his instinctual practice of over-simplifying problems robbed students of the opportunity to engage in productive struggle. He had clear power over this priority because he was the one engaging in this harmful process, regularly.

Another teacher prioritized improved communication with her Spanish-speaking parents. Because she did not speak Spanish, she typically asked her bilingual office staff to make phone calls to parents she did not know how to communicate with. Her lack of direct contact with Spanish-speaking parents guaranteed those parent-teacher-child partnerships would be unacceptably inequitable. But she had the power to change this, because she was the one who had created this not-so-great plan for bridging her language gap.

Focusing on priorities within your scope of power does not mean you give up on the big, impactful fights. Again, because of our preexisting dispositions toward "taking on the man," it is unlikely that you would ever stop fighting the good fight when it comes to issues beyond your scope of power. This involves coalitions, consensus building, and mapping out an external power map to figure out which people can press which buttons to get to your desired change. But if the point of Tangible Equity is to actually address important inequities, you acting within your scope of power allows you to simply follow your personal power map.

Problems

There is nothing like the feeling of setting ambitious goals at the start of the school year. This year, I want 100% of my students to be at or above grade level. This year, I want my students to become self-directed, independent learners. This year, I want to create meaningful, project-based learning experiences to deepen my students' learning at least twice a month.

If I asked you to work with your peers to flesh out these goals, you would almost always start by figuring out the plan for getting there. You want 100% students to be at or above grade level?

You need to look at their current levels and figure how much students need to grow to get there. Want independent learners? You need to plan for how you will create a gradual release model where students will become more comfortable doing the heavy lifting in their learning. You want more meaningful project-based learning? You need to start curating these experiences asap.

But imagine I took a different approach. At or above grade level? These kids? I don't think so. Unless you plan on taking these tests for them, the damage has already been done. Independent learners? Last time I checked, nothing is independent about these kids and all they know how to learn is rap lyrics and TikTok dances. Project-based learning? Here's a project for you: try getting these kids to learn anything, period. That's your project!

Many of us either work or live with this kind of person. The person who shoots down every idea, finds negativity in every goal, and seems to be an all-around hater. This type of reaction is especially tough when you are trying to set up goals that are hard enough without this added negativity. Here you are trying to actually do something about education inequity. You found an important priority that is clearly within your scope of power. What kind of person will kill your hopes and dreams for the future before you even get started?

It turns out, you *need* to be that kind of person to give your priority a fighting chance at success. The third "P" of "*Actually* Doing Something About Educational Inequities" is *Problems* for a very strategic reason: focusing on problems helps us break our psychological connection to our goals. When we set goals, our bias towards wanting to achieve them often leads to a sense of tunnel-vision that prevents us from adequately preparing for foreseeable obstacles. And because few educators want to be "Negative Nancy" colleagues, your colleagues will always favor giving you constructive feedback even when destructive feedback may be more appropriate.

The concept of the pre-mortem is helpful for navigating this shift. You probably know a lot about what a post-mortem is. After someone dies at a hospital from an error, a weird scenario, or other complications, it is obviously helpful to determine what went wrong after the fact. Doctors benefit. Nurses benefit.

Hospital administrators benefit. But do you know who does not benefit? The person who already died!

In a pre-mortem, we free ourselves from the psychological connection to our goals and our fear of being "Negative Nancy" colleagues with a liberating assumption: your goal already failed. Today is the last day of school. That goal you made about bringing 100% to students to at or above grade level did not work. You did not even hit 10%. What happened? Despite your goal that students become these independent, self-directed learners, you have even more help-addicted students than before. What happened? Your goals around regularly-scheduled project-based learning content translated to only one actual project that was a disaster. What happened?

Hindsight is 20/20. It is so much easier for us to honestly critique the goals we did not reach after the fact. This is precisely why the pre-mortem is the recommended approach for improving your success odds with the educational inequity you are prioritizing. As shown in Figure 6.2, it takes three steps to NIP the problems likely to side-track your crucial efforts in the bud:

To apply this, consider my example of unduly harsh discipline towards the Black boys in my class. If I reached the end of the school year and nothing changed—I was still referring Black boys out of class at twice the rate of other teachers—what are the problematic things that likely stood in my way? By "things," I mean policies, procedures (both written and unwritten), structural barriers, or anything that is not a person. In my case, the school's disciplinary policy was a problematic thing. In this pre-mortem scenario, it seems fair to conclude that I could not follow the policy to the letter and also change my practices. Another problematic thing was my teacher evaluation rubric; a teacher

1.	**N**ame the Problematic Things
2.	**I**dentify the Problematic People
3.	**P**rioritize the Problem Over the Things and the People

FIGURE 6.2
Three Steps to NIP Problems.

evaluation framework that placed so much value on a controlled classroom could have incentivized the pushing out of disruptive students. Lastly, my fear likely played a huge role in this failure. If I sat here giving Black boys all sorts of second chances and lots of grace in a harsh world that does not do the same, there is a real fear that I would be doing them a tremendous disservice.

Problematic people are often even more important to name. People can refer to individual people within your various stakeholder groups or to specific individuals. Using the same scenario, I remember receiving tickets for an assembly for the "good kids" (the ones below a certain number of behavior points) and misplacing a ticket. When I walked my class to the assembly, I passed by her office and asked for another one and she berated me in front of my students and made us all wait five minutes after the assembly started to receive the tickets. I can only imagine the wrath that would come my way if she knew I was purposely ignoring her prized behavior system. There were at least two parents who saw me as a baby educator they did not trust with their children. If they labeled me "too lax," somehow this would circle back and end with the behavior lady yelling at me. Clearly, I was petrified of the behavior lady!

My students were a problematic group as well. When I gave my students mid-year surveys to get a pulse on how they thought things were going, I was shocked to see a repeated theme: so many students wanted me to be *more* strict! These middle schoolers were conditioned to teachers who believed in madness like not smiling until Thanksgiving. If I were a fly on the wall in other classrooms my students attended that year, I could guarantee some version of "but in Mr Seale's class I don't get in trouble for ____" was said on a daily basis.

I named the problematic things. I identified the problematic people. But where this work typically falls short is the next, and most important step: ensuring that we hold the line on the problem we are trying to solve as we work to remove obstacles to the unacceptable inequity we committed to change. It is very easy to compromise around inequities that do not personally impact you or your life all that much. This requires setting a clear line in the sand that is non-negotiable.

For instance, imagine serving as your school system's kindergarten coordinator. After several years, you realize that your students from economically disadvantaged backgrounds did not have access to high quality pre-kindergarten programs, struggle in kindergarten, and tend to make up the overwhelming majority of students who are not proficient readers by third grade. You decide that your school system must launch 15 full-day kindergarten programs to meet this need. Your superintendent supports this and has given you the sole power to figure this out. So you have the power, you know the priority, but you have problematic things and problematic people in the way: full-day kindergarten programs are not in the budget, schools are already bursting at the seams and do not have the capacity to add more students, and three out of five board members are hardcore "show me the data" people who are highly skeptical of the benefits of this new initiative.

What would you do? I worked on a group project involving a similar hypothetical scenario, and I felt extremely proud about the proposal my group came up with. To overcome the budget constraints and win over the skeptical board members, we suggested developing a pilot program at two schools in year one, expanding to six in year two, and using our strong success data to support the full launch of all 15 programs. Brilliant plan!

But there was one glaring flaw: we prioritized 15 full-day kindergarten programs because we believed that we could actually do something to reduce the role that demographics play in early elementary academic success by launching 15 full day kindergarten programs. Not two, not six, but 15. Some of you might be thinking that I was "just being realistic." I might have presumed the same thing. It is important to note, however, that we are so conditioned to inequity that unacceptably unjust policies and practices appear "realistic" while necessary improvements to solve real problems appear "unrealistic." If the children struggling in early elementary grades were my children, I would not be okay knowing that an education leader decided that my child had an urgent need for full day kindergarten, but still decided to wait two years to make that option available.

My priority was to launch 15 full-day kindergarten programs. Anything less than that does not fix the priority inequity I want to address. Not enough money in the budget? Maybe I can figure out how much more money it would cost to administer full-day kindergarten and build a coalition of supporters who can advocate for reallocating budget priorities. Maybe I engage the community to find creative ideas for expanding capacity for housing a full day program. Maybe I partner with the local university to write grants to fund this initiative. But under no circumstance will I negotiate against myself by an initial solution that would not even come close to addressing my priority.

Problems are inevitable. But Tangible Equity requires us to hold the line on the priority as we overcome barriers and obstacles. Playing small and being "realistic" are ineffective strategies if the work you wish to do purports to change a system that is not just broken, but intentionally designed to produce the results we see. Transformative work requires a laser focus on the priority at hand. If you go hard and end up with eight schools instead of the 15 you need in year one, at least you know you did all you could to fight for the true need.

Probe

Your priority is an important one. Honestly, there are countless important priorities in our school system. The challenge is, very few priorities actually get addressed until they are both important and urgent. Conducting a Probe, the fourth P, helps you build a sense of urgency around your priority. Urgent issues are "act right now" problems. Urgent issues are the types of issues that cause educators and leaders lose sleep at night. Without establishing both importance and urgency, the constant flood of new, urgent issues educators face will inevitably stall progress on addressing your priority.

When I started thinkLaw, my priority was closing the critical thinking gap so that demographics no longer served as barriers to critical thinking access. No school leader or educator I spoke to downplayed the importance of critical thinking access. But cre-

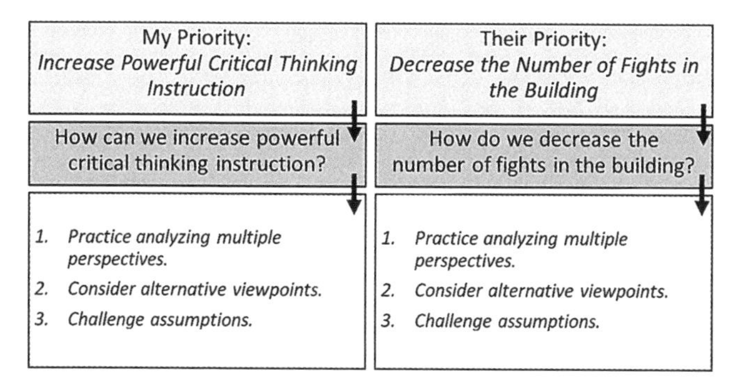

FIGURE 6.3
Sample Probe: Where Do Root Causes Overlap?

ating a sense of urgency around critical thinking access was far more challenging. Early on, this work was often received with a "would be nice" attitude. That was not enough to create a commitment to action. And the truth is, even I would not have had the tenacity to keep pushing for a critical thinking revolution if I, myself, did not understand why this was an urgent challenge.

Conducting an effective probe requires a two-pronged exploration, shown in Figure 6.3: 1) determining the root causes of the issue you are prioritizing and 2) determining how your issue may be an important contributor to other urgent challenges. Probing my unfair disciplinary practices for Black boys, for instance, forces me to ask "why am I doing this?" and "how is what I am doing impacting other urgent issues at my school?"

As I shared earlier, the root cause of my behavior was my explicit bias, my fear, and my normalization of overly harsh, oppressive conduct. How was this an important contributor to other urgent challenges? Well, students can't learn if they are not in class. The vast majority of students I regularly kicked out of class were "bubble" kids; students who failed state exams in the prior year but were very close to passing. Even though my school's disciplinary policy was sacred, nothing mattered more than the success of our "bubble" kids. Conducting this brief probe helped me to ensure that whatever solution I came up with actually addressed the root issues behind my conduct and connected my priority to an important and urgent school priority.

An effective probe also helps you to overcome problems without compromising your priority. I came across many school leaders who saw critical thinking as a "would be nice" solution but obsessed over their urgent need to improve social emotional learning at their schools. Critical thinking became far more urgent once they realized the power of having every student in every grade level analyze different perspectives, consider alternative viewpoints, and challenge assumptions. These are conflict resolution strategies. These are strategies that build empathy. Critical thinking was now tied to an issue that kept those school leaders up at night.

Privilege

Privilege is an interesting word. As a lawyer, it always makes me think about The Privileges and Immunities Clause of Article IV, Section 2 of the Constitution, which states that "the citizens of each state shall be entitled to all privileges and immunities of citizens in the several states."[3] As an educator who cares deeply about equity, it makes me think of the concept of White Privilege, male privilege, and the vast number of demographic classifications and lived experiences that could cause someone to say "check your privilege" to someone who says or does something in a way that appears indifferent to the way these privileges may play out. In essence, privilege is really about being in a position to hold a special advantage, right, or immunity. Leveraging your privilege is a crucial component to actually doing something about educational inequities.

It is often hard for some to fully grasp and find comfort in the notion of White Privilege. And I admit that I often wish a better word than "privilege" was used to explain this concept. I empathize with white people who grew up in the struggle and feel like they had little no special advantages, rights, or immunities because of their race. It is challenging to convince white man born with a disability from a poor, rural community whose family struggled with substance abuse that they benefited from White Privilege." White Privilege is less about the benefits, and more about the reality that of all the systemic barriers you might face, your race is not a significant factor in those barriers.

Male privilege may be a little easier to grasp. In my college Women's Studies course at Syracuse University, I remember an ongoing assignment to maintain a "privilege log." What were my privileges as a Black, cisgendered, heterosexual, able-bodied male? So much of what I wrote in this log used negative words like don't and never. I never have to worry about being harassed in the bathroom because of my gender identity. Racism against Black people is deemed unacceptable enough that I don't have to deal with the reality of several major league teams using mascots and names that mock my race. I don't have to doubt whether a mainstream movie or television show will feature relationships that align with my sexual orientation.

I can go to bar by myself or walk down the street with a mean mug and never have to worry about someone asking me why I am by myself or someone advising me to smile. I went back home to Brooklyn one weekend, and I saw a man on the train in a wheelchair looking closely at the subway map. He needed to confirm the stop he wanted to get off at was wheelchair accessible. The map said it was. But when we got off, another rider and I needed to help him up the stairs because the elevator was broken. I never had to worry about whether I would be physically able to exit at the train station for my destination.

My privilege did not serve as a grand prize to entitle me to this amazing life. It was just a constant reminder that although I did nothing special to earn this, I was immune from certain disadvantages and had access to special advantages that others lacked simply because of who I was. What I am *not* suggesting is that we line ourselves up and ask questions about our privileges and lack thereof, taking steps forwards or steps back so we can feel the shame that comes with both lacking and benefiting from privilege. Instead, the fifth P is all about leveraging your privilege to improve the likelihood of your priority translating into actual change.

The amazing part of privilege is that everyone has it. If you are the fourth generation of your family in your community, you have the privilege of history, connections, and institutional knowledge that helps you get things done. Active in a faith-based organization? A historically Black fraternity or sorority? A neighborhood association? Are you a second-generation educator in your school system? Are you a gym rat with a crazy group of boot camp people who do wild workouts at 5:00 am every day? Maybe you belong to a coalition of LGBTQ educators, a parent group, a car club, or a weekly trivia team. All of these groups come with special privileges, immunities, and advantages.

Leveraging your privilege for change can be as simple as letting someone use your membership card at Costco. But typically, it means a lot more. Leveraging privilege often requires you to use your privilege to do something that has the potential to hurt you in the process. I went through this when I launched Algebra Boot Camp at my school in Washington, DC. I was one of two Algebra I teachers. The other teacher went on jury duty in March and decided to never come back. And I was a first-year teacher worried that our grading scale allowed students to receive a C or better in Algebra I despite receiving grades as low as 40% on the final exam. But I had two important privileges to fix this issue.

First, I spoke to 100% of my families within the first two weeks of school and maintained contact with at least a monthly phone call with all of my families. I had the privilege of trust. They knew I trusted them as experts on their children. They trusted me as someone who showed up before school, stayed after school, and even showed up on Saturdays to support their students. I was the only Black male on my team and the only teacher who was also the child of immigrant parents. My shared identity with this population made the trust even deeper. So, when I asked them to postpone their summer plans and give me two-to-four weeks to work with their children to get them where they need to go, more than 80% of Algebra I students—including students I did not even teach—enrolled and completed the boot camp.

Second, as a Computer Science major, I was active in the National Society for Black Engineers. NSBE was a powerhouse organization with lots of community service requirements. Because I had the privilege of being a NSBE alumni, I had an easy time getting Howard University engineering students to serve as Algebra Boot Camp tutors. I was 22 years old. But to my students, I was "old." 19- and 20-year-old college students? They were "cool." They had privilege, too: the privilege of influence to middle school students.

This example was a relatively simple, comfortable way to leverage my privilege. Your priority might require a deeper level of sacrifice that is complex and uncomfortable. A teacher colleague of mine is a white woman working with a predominately white staff of educators that serve almost entirely students of color. She noticed that at staff meetings, two white men and one white woman frequently interrupted, put down, and "well, actually-ed" Black and Brown women in meetings. Her district cared deeply about recruiting teachers of color, but struggled to retain the few they recruited because of everyday megaaggressions like this (I call them megaaggressions, not microagressions, because there is nothing "micro" about being regularly slighted, overlooked, and underestimated because of your appearance and identity). Leveraging her privileges—the privilege of knowing that a white person pointing out racial justice is more likely to be taken seriously because they will not be presumed to be playing the "race card," her privilege as a respected teacher with experience and clout amongst her peers—she called it out during the next staff meeting when it happened again. And it never happened again.

What did she lose? She informed me that these three teachers gave her the cold shoulder whenever they crossed paths. She also lost the comradery of the gossip cohort of teachers who were now hesitant to engage with messy behavior around her for fear she might similarly call them out. What did she gain? Not a whole lot. The teachers of color did not thank her. They nodded their heads in approval when she made her comment. The net result of her action is that she leveraged her privilege to end an unjust practice and now has to deal with occasional awkwardness and discomfort with a small fraction of her colleagues.

But can we be honest? Occasional awkwardness and discomfort can feel really awful! Growing in Brooklyn, my friends would always make fun of me because of my extreme stance on avoiding awkwardness and discomfort. For instance, if we passed someone while walking and engaged in some small talk while catching up, I was fine. But if, on our way back, I noticed that we were about to pass that person again? Time for a detour. I have no interest in doing that thing where you pass by someone and make an awkward smile or say "hey stranger, long time, no see." I am no different than most educators who find any sort of confrontation tough. Confrontations about inequitable practices are even more tough.

To become proficient at leveraging privilege, you have to practice bravery in advance. One year, I dealt with this concept when teaching Eriq. Eriq was an extremely special human being. He was in my seventh-grade math class, had a severe stutter that led to him being bullied a lot, had a mean right hook that shut up a lot of bullies but got him in a lot of trouble, and was such a hard worker. He started the year about two grade levels behind, but he came to see me every morning before school and every day after school to get caught up, and he was on track to end the year above grade level! What made Eriq even more admirable was the daily struggle he lived through as a child of a parent struggling with alcoholism. Eriq was practically a father figure to his younger brother because his mother was typically passed out by the time he got home from school.

One day, I was wrapping up a meeting with the math department chair who had quasi-authority over me. Right after the meeting, we stood next to each other in the doorway for hall duty. Eriq walks by and happens to have his pants sagging. She yelled out him, "Eriq, pull up your pants!" Like every child called out for a uniform violation, he snickered, rolled his eyes, and begrudgingly complied. As he walked away, she stared at him and said, "that kid is on my shit list."

I was appalled. Infuriated. Immediately, I took her to task. "Are you serious? You are an adult. How dare you say that a child is on your shit list? Do you even know this kid? Do you know that he is not a troublemaker, but defends himself because people bully him since he stutters all the time? Do you know how hard he works in math? This kid is here every day before school and after school and is on track to be above grade level. And his character…do you even know this young man's character? Do you know that he is a father figure to his little brother because his mom struggles with substance abuse? How dare you! You should be ashamed of yourself. And then I stormed off and went back to my classroom.

I was appalled. Infuriated. But the truth is, I am not telling the truth. The truth is that when this leadership figure told me that this kid was on her shit list, I said nothing. I spent the last 16 years thinking about all of the things I should have said, but didn't. I did not say anything because I chose adult comfort over what I knew was best for kids. She was highly influential. If I called her out for her behavior, there was a very good chance I would end up on the same list as Eriq. It did not help that my meeting with her before this incident was all about giving me tools and strategies to improve my instruction, because I was really struggling. Part of me felt too imperfect to criticize her conduct.

What breaks my heart, what makes my inaction haunt me for all this time all this time is the painful conclusion of my journey with Eriq: within two months of this incident, Eriq was expelled from my school for excessive disciplinary consequences. It turns out, he was on her shit list. I could have used this chapter to talk about all the amazing ways I have shown bravery and courage in standing up against inequities. But I think there is so much more you can learn from my inaction. My hope is that you use my shortcomings as a reminder to practice bravery, prepare for the discomfort bravery brings, and recognize that it is never okay to choose adult comfort over what is best for kids.

People

The People component of the Six Ps is not a stand-alone consideration, but an element of all the other five. Naming your power, for instance, must include a reflection on the people you hold positional power over and have strong likelihood of creating influential power with. Your priority almost always impacts other people: students, parents, co-workers, etc. People are almost always an important part of the problems complicating your priority. And leveraging privilege often involves a strategic use of the stakeholders involved in this work.

For instance, a colleague of mine was looking to address the inequitably and disproportionately low representation of Black and Latinx high school students in advanced coursework. The people she initially planned on reaching out to were families of students of color. She planned on having them come out to board meetings to testify to their frustrations about their students' lack of access. After I pushed her on this issue, she chose a different strategy: encouraging white and Asian parents to testify.

Not to say hearing directly from parents of color who felt their children were excluded was a bad thing. But to leverage privilege and people, think about what her all-white board's reaction would be to an angry white or Asian mom saying something like "This is unacceptable. You say you are trying to prepare our students to compete in the 21st century, global workforce. But you throw them in classes where there are almost no Black and Brown students? You are underpreparing my child to deal with the diversity they will see in the workplace and I demand a change." Strategic consideration of people and privilege is a helpful way to support your priority.

One final note on people: think broadly about the people you need involved. Who are the colleagues, families, students, and stakeholders who must be involved? As you explore this, consider direct contacts and connectors—those people who are amazing at helping you get to the people you need to address your priority. Ask yourself, who is missing? In other words, who should be at the table who is not there right now, and if you don't know what you don't know, who can give you the outside perspective to help you bring in who you are not including?

There is no one-size-fits-all framework for addressing inequities. For this reason, The Six Ps are flexible and adaptable to the unique challenges different types of issues involve. Remember that this work exists within a system that is not broken, but designed to produce the outcomes we see. The Six Ps allows educators to be intentional and strategic about addressing inequities—an important counter given the level of intent and strategy involved in creating our inequitable reality.

Notes

1 The Notorious BIG. 1994. *Ready to Die*. Bad Boy—Arista.
2 The Notorious BIG. 1994."Juicy". *Ready to Die*. Bad Boy—Arista.
3 Library of Congress. n.d. "US Constitution—Article IV Accessed October 6, 2021. https://constitution.congress.gov/constitution/article-4/

Bibliography

The Notorious BIG. 1994. *Ready to Die*. Bad Boy—Arista.
The Notorious BIG. 1994. "Juicy". *Ready to Die*. Bad Boy—Arista.

7

Tips for Successfully Implementing and Sustaining Tangible Equity Priorities

In Chapter four, I wrote about my frustration with edu-celebrities who falsely claim that "education has not changed in 100 years." Holding back my throat-punch temptations becomes even harder when these folks give us the solution teachers and education leaders are too dumb to figure out on our own. What is this magical solution? To redesign. To reinvent. And my all-time favorite, to reimagine!

Redesigning, reinventing, and reimagining education does not even make sense. You can design anything. So, isn't redesigning something really just designing something? Same for reinvent…unless you want to "invent" something that has already been invented, tried, and thrown out. And I cannot even try to make sense out of what it would mean to reimagine something. You either imagine something or you don't. Giving the most open-minded interpretation of these verbs, redesigning, reinventing, and reimagining education often refers to making huge, disruptive changes to a system that is oddly resistant to huge, disruptive change.

DOI: 10.4324/9781003282464-10

I can admit if public education did not exist today, it is hard to believe we would decide to structure our education system the way we do right now. We have some weird traditions in education. For instance, we have near-universal agreement that the social-emotional and mental health needs of teenage students are woefully underserved by our outrageously high student-to-counselor ratios. Yet, it is still the norm for high schools across the United States to use our counselors' limited time to design and alter student schedules. The master schedule creates such a powerful barrier to instituting meaningful instructional changes, particularly at secondary levels. From the way we grade to the way we place students in grades based on age as the primary determinant, there is a lot of room for designing, inventing, and imagining (minus the "re") in today's education system.

There is a challenge, however, that frustrated me since I became a baby educator in 2004. Why do so many so-called bold, innovative, and transformational initiatives overlook what actually happens at the classroom level? States and districts across the country have adopted innovative governance models that give some schools and systems greater flexibility. They have designed ambitious "Profiles of a Graduate" laying out all of the skills, habits, and mindsets students should have after completing their K-12 education. School systems also strive to address every hot-button issue as well as they can. School-to-prison pipeline concerns has led many school systems to adopt restorative justice policies, implement positive behavior systems, and add nuance and discretion to some zero-tolerance policies. Concerns around low expectations and low student achievement has led even more states and school systems to hunker down on research-based curriculum and instructional materials, hardcore training requirements on the science of reading, and performance-based teacher evaluations.

For states and school systems prioritizing equity, the list of innovations is even longer. The desire to create a deeper connection between students and their content has led to an explosion in culturally responsive and sustaining education as a priority. This shift is not just about instructional practices, but also about adopting new texts and instructional materials that better reflect the lives and faces of our students. The image from the viral equity graphic of the shortest child needing the most crates to see over the fence to the baseball game has made some impact; most states and districts now provide weighted funding to better meet the needs of students who face greater barriers to academic success. From one-to-one devices to free breakfast, lunch, and dinner for all students in high-poverty school systems, there is no shortage of revolutionary changes in education. Take that, "education hasn't changed in 100 years" folks!

There is a story behind this story, however. I did not understand this story until the massive disruption our education systems faced in the global pandemic. When I first started teaching, I wondered why the 20-plus-year veterans never seemed to blink when we rolled out a new curriculum, a new evaluation framework, or a new testing platform. I wondered why they would chuckle at me when I asked them questions about our new blackboard configuration and how to transfer my lessons into the new lesson plan systems. My immature understanding of education at that time led me to believe the myth of veterans being "stuck in their ways." These veterans were survivors of change after change, initiative after initiative, transformation after transformations. They were not stuck in their ways. They were wise enough to understand and accept that no-one knew the way, period.

I do not want to take this to the extreme and say that teachers should be in charge of everything and be trusted for everything. Education is complex, educating children is complex, and managing that complexity requires management. But there is an important rule implementing policy effectively that so many high-level policy-makers and system-level leaders fail to follow: those closest to the desired change must be meaningfully included in planning and executing that change.

This lesson hit me in my Social Policy graduate class in my Master's in Public Administration Program at Syracuse University's Maxwell School of Citizenship and Public Affairs. Professor David Van Slyke once told us a story about a local county government with a once thriving, now struggling cafeteria. The cafeteria sold food to the county's employees and to members of the general public. But when a new food court opened across the street, most of the cafeteria regulars took their business elsewhere. This is nowhere near the scale of problems in our education system, but there was a problem, nonetheless: what can the county government do to bring some business back to this formerly revenue-generating cafeteria?

The idea that won the day came from the analysts. The analysts surveyed the prices of the food court and the prices of the cafeteria and realized the prices were relatively close. The food options were also somewhat similar. They made their data-driven decision even richer with a few focus groups, gaining valuable qualitative data. After weeks of surveying, data collection, and analysis, the analysts proposed a policy that was immediately adopted. They were after the powers-that-be were highly impressed by the policy, because who wouldn't be impressed with all of this careful data collection and analysis?

The big idea was rather simple: to address the loss of customers at the county cafeteria, the county cafeteria would now start offering 15% discounts to county employees who choose to dine there. This was a significant discount that was supposed to pay for itself with increased foot traffic. And like most initiatives we see with mixed success in education, it worked, somewhat, for a while, until it didn't.

The number of customers initially increased, but this increase did not lead to as much revenue generation as expected. Within a month, the customer traffic leveled out to the same dismal numbers the cafeteria had prior to the implementation of the new policy. What surprised the analysts, however, was that the revenue was even lower than before! Why did something that looked so good on paper fail so miserably in reality?

Because no-one spoke to the person most responsible for successful implementation of the policy: the cashiers! These cashiers had relationships with their regulars whether they worked for the county or were members of the general public. The cashiers were happy to see the increase in business that came from the discount, initially. But they were put in a very awkward position when they had to deny the discount to their cherished regulars who did not work for the county. Within days, the cashiers universally started giving the 15% employee discount to every single customer. Within weeks, the employee discount was no longer a meaningful incentive to dine at the cafeteria. Within a year, the cafeteria closed down.

Education is not a business and should not be run like a business. If education were run like a business, we would be in trouble. 20% of businesses fail in the first year, half fail within five, and two out of every three fail by the tenth year. Education cannot afford to fail. Yet, like this very clever, data-driven, cafeteria improvement policy, too many initiatives in education work, somewhat, for a while, until they don't.

I cannot, for the life of me, understand why someone as crucial to the successful implementation of the cafeteria policy as the cashiers who process the transactions were not considered at any stage of the process. Similarly, I have shadowed Assistant Principals in charge of test administration who spend up to 40 hours manually entering special education and language accommodations into systems that do not communicate with each other—hours they are supposed to be spending supporting teachers in classrooms—and shook my head in empathy as they ask in moments of peak frustration, "Why do they always buy all these systems without our input?" That new, improved, teacher evaluation framework is research-based and much better than the old one. But if principals are not involved meaningfully as evaluators and teachers are not involved meaningfully as the ones being evaluated, you can end up in the common scenario where principals spend more time completing evaluation paperwork (often multiple times a year) than they do in classrooms supporting teachers in the areas noted on the evaluation.

At the teacher level, it is hard to name how many edtech solutions purporting to be helpful for teachers are at best, a solution in search of a problem and at worst, the opposite of helpful. This is a large, expensive challenge. A bombshell analysis of 200,000 curriculum software licenses purchased by 275 schools in the 2017–2018 school year, amounting to two billion dollars in spending, found that two out of three licenses go unused. Some school systems had almost 90% of their software licenses going unused. If this were extrapolated to the $8.4 billion edtech marketplace, this could mean school systems are wasting over five billion dollars a year on products the vast majority of educators are not using.[1]

This is not a call for including teachers for the sake of inclusion. It is a damning, but preventable consequence of failing to prioritize the input, views, objections, and ideas from those closest to the problem. And this is not just about teachers. Students and families are crucial stakeholders in our education system who rarely get consulted for their feedback until decisions have already been made. This may invoke that saying, "if you're not on the table, you're on the menu." But I think we need to push further than this. If you are not strategically designing your table's seating chart with the people holding the expertise that comes from proximity to the problem, they are not going to eat the food!

The entire point of this book is that Tangible Equity requires sustainable transformation at the classroom level. Effectively implementing any change in education is always difficult. Change fatigue, "one-more-thing" syndrome, and the lack of trust that comes from botched efforts of the past do not help matters. But given the urgent need for the Tangible Equity priorities school systems need to see through, every stakeholder involved should advocate that we always make a P-STOP before we go feet-first into the next initiative. A P-STOP, as shown in Figure 7.1, requires us to ensure we focus on the underlying problem at hand and design clear, equitable opportunities to meaningfully engage Students, Teachers, Other people you haven't thought of who matter to the specific issue at hand, and Parents.

P	Problem Identification (ask why)
S	Students
T	Teachers
O	Other People You Haven't Thought of Who Matter to the Specific Issue at Hand
P	Parents

FIGURE 7.1
Make a P-Stop.

For example, imagine you were the professional development coordinator for a district and listened to teachers and principals about the need for more campus level professional development hours to successfully implement important district initiatives. You decide that this is an important equity priority because the campuses with teachers needing the most support tend to serve students who need the same. The principals and teachers are all open and excited about doing what the district across town does: early release Wednesdays, where students are released two hours before school ends every Wednesday. This gives their teachers and administrators 90 minutes of professional time.

STOP! It is time to make sure you name the problem and meaningfully engage students, teachers, other people, and parents in this process. Rapid problem-solving is a necessary evil of a fast-paced education system with lots of time pressure. Even when you do not have lots of time to decide, however, skipping the step of naming the problem can lead to unfocused and ineffective solutions. At the surface, it looks like the problem is "not enough professional development hours to successfully implement important district initiatives." But why? Why is there not enough time? Is it because there is not enough dedicated time for this work? What if the real problem is that there are too many "important" district initiatives. If your boss labels every email as urgent, none of them is urgent. If there are eleven "important" district initiatives, none of them is important. Sometimes, you just have to move forward with a solution even when you believe your school system's understanding of the problem is incorrect. That's where the rest of P-STOP becomes helpful.

Meaningfully engaging with stakeholder groups goes beyond asking for feedback in a survey. It goes beyond asking them if they like or dislike an unproven idea or suggestion. It even goes beyond asking them what their needs are. Legend says that when Henry Ford invented the Model-T, had he asked people about their transportation needs, they would have told him they wanted a faster horse who can ride for longer distances. There are a lot of ifs involved in this type of work, but this Double-If process for meaningfully engaging stakeholders in this work requires just two ifs, as shown in Figure 7.2.

Impact Storytelling	Implementation Considerations
Failure Predications	Future Relief

FIGURE 7.2
Double-If Process.

Impact storytelling allows every stakeholder to answer the question, "why does this problem matter to me?" by explaining how this problem significantly impacts them through stories. A fourth-grade student may not know much about teacher professional development time blocks. But she could tell you that the teacher she looped with from third to fourth grade now seems frazzled, confused, and all over the place with the new curriculum the district adopted this year. A teacher could share that she supported the idea of a more flexible, adaptable curriculum model during the adoption processes last year. But because he has three different classes to prep for, he ends up using the bare minimum, one-size-fits-all curriculum that students do not find too fulfilling.

Other people who matter to this issue? The instructional technology staff can tell you stories of how they have no time to proactively address cyber-security and roll out new parent communication technologies because they are struggling to answer questions teachers have about software neither group has been trained in that well. School counselors might tell you about the growing number of students complaining that their teachers do not know their names or anything about them. And parents might tell you that the new curriculum resources your district bought to better support teachers do not have enough student-facing information, leading them to feel like pests to their children's teachers who are already strained to the max.

Failure predictions start with you naming your proposed solution and asking, "why will this NOT work." There are few audiences more skeptical than education stakeholders. When you ask them to voice objections, you typically will not have to ask twice. Frame this question by naming the idea, followed by "why will this not work." In the case of this early release Wednesday, say, "I want to give teachers additional professional learning time by letting students out two hours early every Wednesday. Why will this NOT work?

Countless design considerations of our Tangible Equity program came from failure predictions with hundreds of conversations with school system leaders, principals, instructional coaches, educators, students, and parents over an 18-month period. We work with teachers to transform their existing curriculum so it does not feel like "one more thing." We align our strategies and instructional models to existing district priorities, frameworks, and evaluations so our work is always complementary, never contradictory to expectations that are already there. We train parents and families in key aspects of Tangible Equity because parents and families are key levers of power districts rarely leverage for change. Failure predictions taught us to fix potentially fatal problems before they broke.

Implementation considerations are a close friend to failure predictions. The question here is also simple: I remember launching thinkLaw with just a few lessons written in Microsoft Word and thinking that critical thinking lessons based on real-life legal cases could be an amazing resource for schools serving youth in juvenile detention settings. Without question, many incarcerated youth are critical thinkers who typically find themselves in square peg, round hole situations in the traditional classroom. Luckily, a former colleague of mine from my child welfare days was now the deputy director of the juvenile detention center schooled me to a basic design consideration: no prerequisites, please!

He complained to me extensively about how many evidence-based programs they adopted that required every session be completed in a specific sequence. This was a massive pain point for their transitory youth population, forcing them into annoying holding patterns where no-one could start these programs until the current cohort completed all their sessions. Fortunately, I only had three lessons designed in Microsoft Word! It was easy to incorporate this advice into the design of the thinkLaw curriculum going forward, much easier than if I did what we do in education all the time and pushed forward without getting this type of implementation advice.

The questions here can vary. "_____ is my proposed solution to this problem. What configuration of this solution would work best given your context?" Another one is "Have you experienced a similar solution in the past?" Or "What lessons learned from implementing that solution can help us be more successful now?" Essentially, any question that leads you to gather very specific feedback about specific aspects of your specific solution is a good one.

The last, but most important aspect of the Double-If process is something I call future relief. The premise of future relief is that right now, stakeholders may feel lots of pressure and anxiety about the problem they are grappling with. By asking them to consider, "what it would look like if this solution was an overwhelming success" or even better, "what would it *feel* like if this solution was an overwhelming success," you get stakeholders to articulate, in very clear terms, what your solution's changed reality means to them.

Note

1 Davis, Michelle R. 2019. "K-12 Districts Wasting Millions by Not Using Purchased Software, New Analysis Finds." Market Brief. May 14, 2019. https://marketbrief.edweek.org/marketplace-k-12/unused-educational-software-major-source-wasted-k-12-spending-new-analysis-finds/

Part III

The Five Tangible Equity Philosophical Shifts

8

Classroom Level Philosophical Shifts for Tangible Equity

There is no shortage of inequities to address in education. Part I of this book focused on Tangible Equity, generally, because if educators used RACK (Reflect, Acknowledge, Change, and Keep reflecting, acknowledging and changing) to notice when inequities need to be addressed and the Six Ps to manage the process of actually addressing it, we would see much more actionable version of equity in our schools than what we are used to. Part II walked through some of the powerful, but practical "how" shifts to our approach in education necessary to support this change.

But Part III is all about a specific priority: giving teachers powerful mindset shifts to be disruptive on purpose and disruptive *with* a purpose. In lieu of hard-to-define, hard-to-implement buzzwords, this section discusses five Tangible Equity philosophies to guide the necessary transition to help students adopt the play the game and slay the game approach of the Tangible Equity Equation.

DOI: 10.4324/9781003282464-12

9

Beyond Relationships

Teachers usually like kids, obviously. So why am I stating the obvious? I am stating the obvious because even though teachers typically like, care about, and enjoy lots of things about the students they serve, so many education conversations talk about "relationships" as the key to just about everything. Not that I would ever argue that teachers should not be warm, supportive, understanding, and caring. But what if educators are miss something beyond relationships?

Rita Pierson's viral TED talk may explain this focus on relationships. Her often-quoted statement that "kids can't learn from teachers they don't like" is probably true to some extent.[1] But there is a lot of over-simplification here, and even more questions. As a child, I "liked" teachers who were loose with the rules, did not give us too much work, and made everything easy. I did not learn much from these teachers, which makes me wonder how important liking teachers is to learning.

I also remember teachers like my middle school Earth science teacher who was the epitome of all the boring, awful teachers from television shows like Saved by the Bell and The Wonder Years. I can still smell that regrettable combination of cigarette smoke and teacher's lounge coffee. I can still see the bright yellow stains on the armpits of his dress shirts. Besides all that,

DOI: 10.4324/9781003282464-13

he was completely unapproachable and I often wondered if he even liked children! Yet, somehow, almost 100% of his students passed the high school Earth Science Regents exam—New York City's rigorous state final exam—as eighth graders.

From a research standpoint, no institutional review board or school system would ever approve a study that had teachers be unlikeable on purpose. If students supposedly cannot learn from teachers they do not like, a definition of what it means to "like" a teacher should be helpful.

In *Liking or Disliking the Teacher: Student Motivation, Engagement and Achievement*,[2] support is found for the instinctual idea that students who like their teachers report greater levels of motivation and engagement in those teachers' classrooms. Also unsurprisingly, this study also tied liked teachers to improved achievement. This study's definition of "like" was far less instinctual. Instead of just asking students what teachers they liked and measuring their performance in the classed of liked teachers, they asked students to answer questions from *The Survey on High School Student Motivation* from the perspective of how they feel about those questions based on their experiences in in the liked teachers' classrooms. The study also asked students to complete this survey based on how it related to their disliked teachers.

The findings of this study suggest that relationships are less about relationships alone, and more about relational instruction. Liked teachers created classroom environments with constructive, confidence-building feedback. These learning environments prioritized student interest and collaborative learning. Liked teachers also helped students make meaning out of learning as part of their pathways to achieve their future goals. It is unsurprising, therefore, that students reported higher levels of persistence, exerted greater effort, and earned higher grades in classes when they liked the teacher.

But this is not really about liking their teachers. It is about students liking the learning the teacher facilitates. My Earth Science teacher was not likeable under our traditional understanding of positive student-teacher relationships because he was not warm, kind, understanding, or supportive. But his expectations for us were through the roof. Most lessons tied back to things we could observe with our own eyes in our own neighborhoods of Brooklyn, New York. His lab assignments were open-ended and surprisingly, fun! We spoke more in his class than any other class because he was not particularly interested in answering our questions. He wanted us to answer them ourselves.

He was not fun. But he made learning fun. He was not particularly caring. But he made us care about learning. He was not very supportive or helpful. But he taught us to support each other and help ourselves through his student-centered learning model.

So when I read something like Education Trust's paper, *The Importance of Strong Relationships*, I need to ask, what exactly is a strong relationship? It worries me that in the large, diverse district they surveyed, less than 33% of middle school students had a strong relationship with their teachers—a number that dropped to 16% for 12th graders and was lower, overall, for students from low-income backgrounds. But it encourages me to see that this report similarly fleshed out the instructional pieces of teacher-student relationships. The five components of how to build developmental relationships were expressing care, challenging growth, providing support, sharing power, and expanding possibilities. Educators must care for and support their students. Care and support alone, however, are insufficient without that challenge factor, without intentional spaces for children to unleash their inherent power, and ensuring students learn what they need in and beyond their classrooms.

Adding depth to our understanding of teacher-student relationships is a crucial prerequisite for Tangible Equity. Reducing the predictive power of demographics on outcomes requires a RACK (Reflect, Acknowledge, Change, and Keep Reflecting, Acknowledging and Changing) process for relationships. Specifically, educators should reflect on how student demographics may relate to the type of teacher-student relationships students receive.

A 2018 study sorted relationships into two buckets. An *instrumental focus*, that "were structured as a controlled means to a particular end: student compliance." In this relational model, "[s]tudents learned that their value was tied to the degree to which they worked hard and behaved in line with what mostly white authority figures demanded." The second bucket was a *reciprocal focus*, with "students affirming and responding to their thoughts and experiences. Such interactions prepared them to engage with authority figures, and to someday hold positions of authority themselves."[3]

I see a *reciprocal focus* in the most effective, gifted and talented classrooms I observe. But in the classrooms of some of the highest-performing teachers at some of the highest-performing schools serving economically disadvantaged Black and Brown children, the *instrumental focus* model of relationships tends to dominate. This matched with study findings concluding that teachers trained in the instrumental focus were more likely to teach in schools with mostly low-income students of color, while those trained in the reciprocal focus were more likely to teach in high-income, white students.

"Kids don't learn from teachers they don't like" does not mean educators should strive to be likeable. Relationships matter, but the learning relationship is what really matters. The Learning Relationship Triangle, a model I created as Figure 9.1, places students at the center of it all. I refer to students as Thinkers on purpose, because explicitly naming thinking as a core aspect of

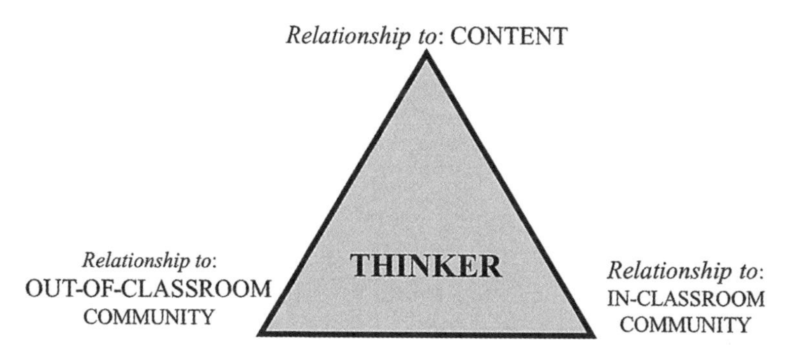

FIGURE 9.1
The Learning Relationship Triangle.

learning reminds educators that student learning is maximized when students experience high levels of cognitive demand.

The Learning Relationship Triangle defines three aspects of the learning relationship. First, how teachers connect thinkers to the content. Second, how teachers create spaces for thinkers to connect to their classroom community of thinkers. Third, how teachers help thinkers connect their learning to skills, issues, and challenges existing beyond the classroom walls.

In the following chapters, you will receive powerful, but practical ideas and strategies for bringing The Learning Relationship Triangle alive in your classrooms.

Notes

1 Pierson, Rita. 2013. "Every Kid Needs a Champion." *TED Talk*. https://www.ted.com/talks/rita_pierson_every_kid_needs_a_champion

2 Montalvo, Gregory P., Eric A. Mansfield, and Raymond B. Miller. 2007. "Liking or Disliking the Teacher: Student Motivation, Engagement and Achievement." *Evaluation & Research in Education* 20 (3): 144–58. https://doi.org/10.2167/eri406.0

3 Theisen-Homer, Victoria Marie. 2018. Teaching for Human Connection: Relationships, Race, and the Training of Teachers. Doctoral diss., Harvard Graduate School of Education.

10

The Top 10% Rule

Almost every working professional has experienced a moment where a boss has a not-so-bright idea to make "non-negotiable" anonsensical policy or practice. Rarely are you ever free to boo loudly and belligerently convey your opposition to the nonsense. But feel free to use all that repressed frustration for your initial response to The 10% rule.

To kick off this school year, your superintendent opens the big opening convocation with a new mandate: The 10% Rule. This rule is straightforward: from now on, you are to teach in such a way that the top 10% of students in your classrooms get their butts kicked, daily. Yes, you heard that right. You have one job. The students who are in your top 10% of academic achievers, your high-fliers, your students with their highest GPAs—these students will all leave your classrooms every day saying, "Wow, that was tough!"

Cue the objections. Think about some of the most likely objections to this wild top 10% strategy. If this were a game of Family Feud, the number one answer would likely be some version of "other students will get left behind." Choosing to challenge the top 10% sounds like ignoring the needs of the other 90%. Struggling students will become extremely discouraged. How do we expect the English Learners, the students with

DOI: 10.4324/9781003282464-14

exceptional learning needs, and students who start the year below grade level to keep up? And let's not forget an important stakeholder group who is definitely not going to be okay with this nonsense: parents!

This Top 10% idea came from a misunderstanding. As hard as it is to admit, there was once I time where I was not fully paying attention during back-to-school professional development. Just that one time, I promise. The leader of my school, a passionate, loud, instruction-obsessed New Jersey native by the name of Michael Piscal, started drawing all these bell curves. He wanted us to understand that when we teach to the middle, we maintain things as the way they are. But if we can shift the bell curve, and start teaching to the top third of the class, we will change what it means to be a mediocre student. At that time, a mediocre student was barely graduating from high school. But if we shifted to teaching to the top 33%, a mediocre student would graduate from a state university.

Somehow, I heard Piscal's directive as a challenge to teach in a way that the top 10% of students would get their butts kicked, daily in my class. Parent pushback was swift:

> My child has always done well in math until stepping into Mr Seale's class.
>
> What is with all this hard work my kid is bringing home from Mr Seale's class? Most of it isn't even math, it's writing!
>
> Mr Seale is crazy to be giving my kid work like this.

Honestly, these complaints were pretty accurate. It was fairly common for students in schools I taught in to earn good grades when they were well-behaved, neat, polite, and compliant, even if they did not actually show mastery of understanding content. It was also true that my habit of having students write a paragraph about what is happening in a graph from the perspective of a girl riding a bicycle was very different than problem sets students were used to. And the truth was, I was definitely crazy—crazy like a fox!

Instead of complaining about this Top 10% strategy as a reckless decision, let's explore a different question: what are the

Top 10% of achievers typically good at? Where do they tend to excel? It turns out, these are students who are exceptional at the game of playing school. They can comply like nobody's business. If you give them an algorithm, they can follow the algorithm. Give them definitions, they can memorize them. Give them rules, they can adhere to them. When they get classwork, they can do homework that looks like the classroom and ace tests that look like both.

Challenging the Top 10% means we must name where the Top 10% is most likely to struggle. Intuitively, we can think of those high-performing students who have a hard time grappling when learning gets funky. Learning where there is no clear black or white answer. Managing learning that involves, drama, confrontation, creativity, ingenuity. As a law student, I remember learning the rule of thumb for predicting future career success: A students become judges, B students work at fancy law firms, C students become rich!

There is something to be said for the conflict between conformity required to achieve in traditional academic spaces and the originality students need to transcend the norm. Being the valedictorian is still an honor. But we have created a space where extraordinary academic achievement has its limits. A study on top achievers found that valedictorians "typically settle into the system instead of shaking it up."[1] When we are trying to reduce the predictive power that demographics have on outcomes, we cannot afford to have our highest achievers be the most likely to settle for the system we have when they are uniquely qualified to help us create the system we ought to have. Using drama, funk, controversy, and conflict to create more of a challenge for students achieving at the top 10% level helps them translate what we tend to call "book smart" to functional, transferable skills.

That said, no-one would rally behind something as disruptive as The Top 10% strategy if there were not clear benefits to the remaining 90%. I cannot frame these benefits without calling out what has come to feel like a four-letter-word in education: differentiation. Differentiation is one of those concepts that makes so much sense in theory but has such little grounding in practical reality. I wish it were a special, rare, once-in-a-lifetime occurrence that my eighth grade classroom had students whose math abilities ranged from third- to tenth-grade levels of proficiency, but these ranges are not uncommon. How is anyone supposed to differentiate instruction with such broad ranges of gaps?

Fortunately, some scholars have researched a modified form of ability tracking that narrows achievement bands within a classroom. Intuitively, it makes sense that two groups of eighth grade students could probably move the needle a lot further if those performing at a third-fifth-grade level were grouped together and those performing at a sixth-eighth-grade level were grouped together. Still, we cannot talk about a Top 10% strategy without naming the elephant in the room: differentiation does not typically include them.

It makes all the sense in the world that overwhelmed and underresourced educators would spend the bulk of their limited time thinking about differentiating for struggling learners. I have never met an audience of educators hostile to my belief that, generally speaking, differentiation is practically interpreted by teachers as doing whatever has to be done so students who are behind do not fall too far behind. This typically means we teach to the "middle," ignore the "top," and support the "low."

Differentiation outside of federally-mandated differentiation required under federal laws for special education is so complex in practice that many educators decide to do the same thing for "all students." "All" often refers to the imaginary middle student. But in reality, "all" means no-one at all. "All" makes the unique needs of individual students invisible. If we truly wish to obtain Tangible Equity, we must shift from "all" to "each." It may seem like mission impossible to design learning experiences that teach and reach each child, but at least this is the right mission. This may be surprising to some, but designing instruction to challenge the Top 10% of traditional academic achievers is key strategy for simplifying differentiation and transitioning from "all" to "each"

Incorporating drama, funk, controversy, and conflict into instruction is a concrete way to engage the other 90% in deeper learning experiences they rarely have the privilege to access. English Learners will dig deep for the academic language needed to engage in the rigorous debate over whether a taco is a sandwich. Struggling learners have a much stronger "why" for engaging in rigorous math content when the lesson on multiplying using money in decimal form is enhanced with a real-world question about whether punitive library fines are worth it—both in financial terms and in terms of how our society suffers when the public cannot use library resources due to unpaid fines.

I consider questions like these to be natural differentiators. These are culturally responsible differentiators because they all invoke some sense of a gut reaction. Your gut reaction is not often referred to as an example of critical thinking. But if I ask you whether a taco is a sandwich, there is a reason you make a judgment call of yes or no. We often hear gut feelings referred to as some sort of sixth sense. But in reality, gut feelings are so much more. They are a combination of all of your five senses plus your identity, your culture, your experiences, your values, and your prior education—both inside and outside of the school building. Gut feelings become an important piece of the critical thinking process when we can name our gut feeling, understand the subjective bias that leads us to adopt that gut belief, and spend our time as learners understanding how to disprove that gut feeling.

Educators practicing a top 10% strategy ask for gut feelings all the time. I observed an advanced placement literature class, for instance, where before diving into a Socratic seminar, the teacher asked students "what is the point of having discussions?" It may not seem like much, but that simple question allowed students to frame their own "why" and get the level of buy-in needed to grapple with the inherent funk that comes from a conversation with no clear right or wrong answers.

A top 10% strategy is not just for honors, advanced placement, gifted, or international baccalaureate classes. I observed a pre-calculus class where I was pleasantly surprised to see almost every student getting almost every question correct on a complex worksheet on function composition. This may bring up mathematical trauma for those of us engaged in the blasphemous, but common practice of saying "I don't do math," but bear with me.

Functions themselves are not hard for most students. It is like a machine in a factory. My high school math teacher taught them to me as "f-machines." Teenagers learn better with f-words, I guess. But the concept is simple: something like $f(x) = 2x + 3$ means that I can put any x-value into my f-machine, like five, and just "plug it in" into the equation via substitution. The result would be $f(5) = 2(5) + 3$, or 13. Composition functions take on another layer.

F of g of x, or $f(g(x))$ means that I take the result of the g-machine and "plug it in" to the f-machine. So if $g(x) = x + 5$, and $f(x) = 2x + 3$, $f(g(5))$ would require me to start with the inner function $g(5)$. This means $g(5) = (5) + 5$, or 10. I would then take that result of 10 and plug it into my f-machine, $f(10) = 2(10) + 3$, getting to 23 as my final answer. A different result would come from doing $g(f(10))$, because using the inner function would get me to $f(5) = 2(5) + 3$, or 13. Then plugging in 13 into my g-machine would lead to $g(13) = (13) + 5$, or 18.

You can imagine that as functions become more complex and start including wacky stuff like $f(g(h(i(x))))$, things can start getting pretty tricky. Yet, this first-year teacher had students rocking out on these problems, even though these were not students known to do particularly well in math generally, and this is usually a tough unit, specifically. Somehow, this first-year teacher had the insight to spark their learning with an issue more controversial than abortion, gun rights, transgender athletes, and assisted suicide combined: whether it is acceptable to put pineapple on pizza.

For some reason I cannot pretend to understand, your take on whether pineapple on pizza is appropriate or unconscionable seems to be pretty important. Discrimination is generally disfavored in society, at large. But I have been publicly shamed and ridiculed by strangers who see the pineapple and sausage pizza my kids love. They did not call child protective services on me, but they questioned what kind of father allows children to commit the moral atrocity of putting pineapple on pizza. Meanwhile, those who indulge in pizza topped with pineapple do so pridefully, daring anyone who opposes their life choices to "come at me bro."

Most precalculus classes do not start with any sort of divisive issue, much less a humorous one like pineapple on pizza. But if this were not actually a pizza, but a pizza machine, this can be a valuable image for composition functions. We can easily think of the idea that you can label a pizza machine as f(x), where x is the quantity of a specific toppings on a pizza. A pineapple machine where g(x) is the quantity of pineapple pieces. And I can think of f(g(x)) as plugging in a certain quantity of pineapple pieces to get the total number that will be on the pizza, and f(g(x)) of putting those slices on the pizza itself. So what would g(f(x)) look like? A war crime, apparently. This would mean you would be taking a huge vertical slice of pineapple and placing little pieces of pizza on that slice. Unless you want to raise serial killers, I strongly advise against feeding such a preposterous meal to any child.

The Top 10% Rule brings funk to instruction and uses *who* our kids are as an accelerant to their learning. It is special that so many students were able to use the idea of pineapple on pizza and pizza on a pineapple to understand composition of functions. But what about an extension where instead of explaining the concept through the pizza example, students had to use a cultural dish, a personal interest, or hobby to explain this concept.

Arroz con pollo is one thing. What would it look like as Pollo con Arroz? Playing basketball where f(x) represents the points I score in a game and g(x) represents the points my team score makes sense as g(f(x)). But what would that mean as f(g(x))? I look at what my team scores, and then plug that into a function involving subtraction to compute my score?

Either way, students would be able to experience deeper learning in a topic that has now become naturally differentiated by allowing students with all sorts of experiences and identities to connect pre-calculus to their lives. In a book called Tangible Equity, you might expect me to say that pre-calculus teachers should work to design lessons based on race and social justice. But the reality is, pre-calculus is out there! Pre-calculus problems are so algorithm-heavy, reliant on vast levels of background knowledge, and highly abstract.

Educators often find the same challenges with designing real-world applications to elementary level grammar, high school chemistry, or advanced concepts in music. No-one can expect that every lesson, every day, will be meaningful, fulfilling learning experiences that give our students the opportunity to change the world. Conjugating verbs in French class means you are conjugating verbs in French class. The quadratic formula is the quadratic formula. But when you can use something as simple as a five-minute exploration of whether people who eat pineapple on pizza should be burned at the stake, you can change students' stake in their learning, lighting said stake on fire.

Teaching to challenge the top 10% of traditional achievers is a concrete equity strategy. Principals and instructional coaches may be working around the clock to support teachers in teaching with "more rigor" and with "high expectations," but those phrases are not very clear. Few teachers would ever openly admit to having low expectations. More likely, educators would say that they set *realistic* expectations for their students. Recalling Chapter five, where I applied the RACK process to data-driven instruction, it is east to see how a fourth-grade teacher with only a handful of students on or above grade level would teach in a *realistic* way. "Teaching to the middle" may mean that students will never have access to rigorous, grade-level work. But teaching to the top 10% is a concrete framework to ensure this access exists.

Issues with access and connectivity existed long before the COVID-19 pandemic forced educators to grapple with access to working devices and broadband connectivity. The top 10% strategy ensures that students have *access* to rigorous, grade-level content. Using funk, drama, controversy, and conflict to deepen learning experiences for all students creates *connections* to content, to other students, and to the world beyond the classroom that align with the previous chapter's Learning Relationship Triangle. Use the Top 10% rule because Tangible Equity cannot ever be realized at the classroom level if students are not regularly given the tools to lead, innovate, and break the things that must be broken.

Note

1 Grant, Adam. 2018. "Opinion—What Straight-A Students Get Wrong." *The New York Times*. December 8, 2018. https://www.nytimes.com/2018/12/08/opinion/college-gpa-career-success.html

11

From Closing Achievement Gaps to Shattering Achievement Ceilings

Take a moment to imagine an educator you know who is the biggest proponent of "these kids can't." This educator, even if she is a figment of your imagination, has consistently low expectations for struggling learners because of every excuse in the book. They are too poor, too slow, too low, too poorly parented, too traumatized to learn.

What do you think would change about this educator if she were told that this school year, she caught a "break" and was now going to be assigned to teach the top 1% of profoundly academic and intellectual gifted students in your state. How do you think this might change the way this teacher prepares for class? How would this change her reactions to students who may misbehave? Could you see this teacher making a different set of assumptions and responding with a different set of actions if a student performed poorly on a test?

There is something about knowing that this kind of teacher would be more thoughtful in preparation, exploring lots more examples, making deeper connections, and going deep into the

DOI: 10.4324/9781003282464-15

academic content and natural extensions of that content. Why is it so instinctual to presume that this teacher would respond to misbehavior and underachievement with a greater sense of personal responsibility? Because despite being the "these kids can't" teacher, when you put her in a situation where she is teaching the top 1% of intellectually and academically gifted students, there is an underlying presumption that "these kids can." This is the premise for a much-needed shift from closing achievement gaps to shattering achievement ceilings.

I often get the side-eye when I mention gifted education and equity in the same sentence. Here is a simple, three-part premise to frame how I view gifted education.

1. All students have gifts and talents.
2. Some, but not all, students are academically gifted and talented.
3. The current population of students we identify as academically gifted and talented is unacceptably whiter and wealthier than the actual student population of academically gifted and talented students should be.

I do not anticipate much disagreement with my first point about all students having unique gifts and talents. Classroom teachers would not dispute my second point about the existence of out-of-this-world brilliant students who are rarely challenged by the content and instruction delivered in the standard classroom environment. Whether we choose to meet, or even *acknowledge* these students' needs, however, often depends on our comfort level with labeling children based on their advanced academic needs—an inconsistent objection given all the ways public education sorts and labels children in just about every other context. And my last point is indisputable: Advocates and experts have highlighted the stubbornly persistent equity issues in gifted education for decades.[1]

It is not surprising that school system leaders prioritizing equity would want to do something about the inequities in gifted education. My concern is that more and more of these leaders are doing the wrong thing. Across the nation, school systems are limiting or eliminating their gifted education and advanced academic offerings.

On the surface, this seems logical. If I'm leading a system where the population of eighth graders taking Algebra I has a disproportionate number of white and Asian students, then eliminating eighth-grade Algebra I as an offering looks like an obvious pathway to equity. According to this way of thinking, shutting down gifted education and selective magnet programs that struggle with a similar gap, in which the program demographics are not even close to representative of the overall student demographics, seems equally wise. But like so many leading equity scholars of color in gifted education research[2] I disagree with these approaches and favor a more expansive solution.

I agree that it is unacceptable to have eighth-grade Algebra I classes and gifted education programs that do not reflect the demographic makeup of the general student population." But if equity is the goal, we should be mandating that every eighth grader takes Algebra I, and structure the entire Pre-K to seventh-grade student experience to ensure this is a legitimate possibility for every child. Since when does equity mean everyone gets nothing?

I do not doubt the good intentions behind the decisions educators make in the name of equity. I see a problem, however, with the outcomes associated with decisions made with harmless intentions but harmful impact. This is personal to me as a child who struggled with excessive behavior challenges in kindergarten and first grade until I was identified as gifted and learned what too many students like me never have the privilege of learning: my behavior challenges came from a lack of being challenged. How many brilliant students without access to gifted programs become disengaged and disruptive because no-one prioritized their special needs?

If equity is the concern, we should also name the inequitable reality that parents with means will always find a way to ensure their children receive whatever out-of-school enrichment resources their children need. My greatest concern? The false notion that school systems can fully implement an "all kids are gifted" framework that attempts to address the issue for eliminating the need for specialized gifted programming.

In my work with thinkLaw (https://thinklaw.us), I lead our efforts to support school systems across the nation to deliver the type of instruction that is typically reserved for gifted and talented learners. But there is a big a difference between a "gifted instruction for all" and an "all kids are gifted" approach. Most states have specific definitions for which children are considered "gifted," which typically include an acknowledgement that these children require specialized services—that are not provided in the general education classroom—to thrive. This requires a child-driven approach, and a one-size-fits-all model for instruction will not meet the unique needs of gifted learners.

For identified and should-have-been-identified gifted students of color, these needs are even more specialized. When teachers do not understand that gifted learners can struggle mightily with underachievement, especially in underrepresented populations, they cannot provide the tools and services needed to address this need. If teachers do not understand the "gifted, and" complexities of identifying and serving English Language Learners, students receiving special education services, and children of undocumented families, they are all but guaranteed to leave all this brilliance on the table. But if we keep eliminating, instead of expanding, gifted programs for populations who need these the most, there will be no table, period, for anyone.

It has never been more important to ensure that students most impacted by our society's inequities are not just getting what they need to be successful academically. We must expand gifted programs and create them where they do not exist to ensure students receive the tools they need to lead, innovate, and break the things that must be broken. This way, we will ensure stories of brilliant students of color breaking through unjust systems are no longer exceptions to the rule but rather have a real shot at achieving truly exceptional academic heights.

When this gap is present, decision-makers must, at a minimum, do an exhaustive analysis of how this decision may be helpful and harmful to the stakeholder group. This is not a substitute for authentic engagement and collaboration. But even for planning purposes prior to having these conversations, some level of thoughtful reflection and acknowledgement that all decisions impact different stakeholder groups in different ways is necessary.

If I were a Black eighth grader who was not currently enrolled in Algebra I, the decision to stop offering Algebra I does not dramatically help or hurt me. It does not help me because I was not taking Algebra I to begin with. And it might actually hurt me for the same reason that a Black student currently enrolled in Algebra I may be hurt. Placing students in my math class who are academically advanced enough to start high school courses may turn my classroom into a space where the advanced learners are disengaged and become disruptive, behavior challenges that are common when students experience a lack of actual challenge.

If I turn my attention to an eighth grader enrolled in Algebra I whose family has the financial means to seek advanced math offerings outside of school, this student's level of hurt from eliminating the program is minimized. Meanwhile, current and potential Algebra I eighth graders without those means will feel this hurt more deeply because if schools did not offer advanced math, they simply would not have access to it anywhere.

Before conducting the stakeholder analysis on the idea of redesigning a school system so that all students will have access to Algebra I in eighth grade, I want to point out an interesting feature of gifted education that would disrupt the deficit-based notion of many of our education conversations. Suppose you were that same "these kids can't" teacher who struggled with low expectations for students I mentioned earlier. How would your mindset be impacted if you were told that next year, 100% of your students will be profoundly gifted academically?

It is easy to see how this would push an educator to prepare differently. Knowing that your students are academically gifted would force you to double down on your content knowledge, ensuring you were ready to grapple with depths and complexities of your lesson that may come up proactively. You know that gifted learners require high levels of engagement, so you would probably do a bit more to get to know your students' interests and passions to incorporate them into your instruction. What would happen if you saw one of your brilliant students struggling academically? I could only imagine that any gap between my gifted learners' potential and their performance would be a "me" problem, causing me to collaborate with the students and their families to fix the clearly ridiculous idea of having a brilliant learner fail on my watch. If a student was disruptive and misbehaving in class? Again, I would own this because clearly, the problem cannot be placed on this brilliant child in front of me. Instead, I must not have created enough purposeful disruption in my lesson to allow this student's natural gifts and abilities to shine through.

An asset-based mindset is hard to define. But when I talk about "teaching to the top," which includes everything from delivering instruction so that the top 10% of learners in every classroom are deeply challenged daily to designing school systems so that all students are ready to take and succeed in eighth-grade Algebra I, this "teach them as if you knew they were gifted" mindset adds a level of specificity that is drastically needed education's jargon-filled universe.

The stakeholder analysis for offering Algebra I to all eighth graders will have the same players. But when I analyze the helpful and harmful impact to the stakeholder group, the outcome looks far different than the elimination decision. Now, current and potential eighth-grade Algebra I students do not see their circumstance changed. If anything, they receive the benefits of being in a more diverse learning environment, the same learning environment they already experienced and clearly thrived in prior to being in the more exclusive eighth-grade Algebra I class. Now, eighth graders who would not have previously qualified to take Algebra I in eighth grade will now have the opportunity to. This group may face temporary hurt because, let's be real, lots of kids experience a knee-jerk "this is hard" reaction to enhanced rigor. But when "this is hard" transforms into "this is normal," students tend to rise to the level of expectation.

Who would be hurt by an eighth-grade Algebra 1 for all policy? The "these kids can't" educators who believe that some eighth graders are simply not "Algebra I material." And by hurt, these educators are not actually going to be hurt. It's just going to require a similarly ambitious lift to help them transform from "these kids can't" to being able to create the learning structures, classroom culture, and pedagogical practices to build the conditions such that "all kids can." The "teach them as if you knew were gifted" mindset can be a powerful prerequisite for aiding in this transition.

It has never been more important to ensure that our students most impacted by our society's inequities are not just getting what they need to be successful academically, but receiving the tools they need to lead, innovate, and break the things that must be broken. This calls for equitable solutions that acknowledge unjust systems and boldly attack these systems to make them fairer. Our country's lack of teacher diversity, for instance, is outrageous, given our student demographics. This gap is even greater in gifted education. I recently launched The BEE Project, a radical solution to create a new reality by paying existing educators of color to earn their gifted educated endorsement so they can teach, lead, and in many cases start new gifted programs in their school systems. I know that radical disruption is easier said than done in a system that rewards compliance and craves smooth waters. But if what you are doing seems comfortable, there's a good chance it is not equity work.

Notes

1 Brasher, Joan. 2018. "Donna Y. Ford Honored for Commitment to Desegregation of Gifted Education." Vanderbilt University. March 30, 2018. https://news.vanderbilt.edu/2018/03/30/donna-y-ford-honored-for-commitment-to-desegregation-of-gifted-education/

2 Ford, Donna Y., Kenneth T. Dickson, Joy Lawson Davis, Michelle Trotman Scott, and Tarek C. Grantham. 2018. "A Culturally Responsive Equity-Based Bill of Rights for Gifted Students of Color." *Gifted Child Today* 41 (3): 125–29. https://doi.org/10.1177/1076217518769698

12

Low Floor, High Ceiling

In late August 2021, China instituted major restrictions on online gamers under the age of 18. China limited their weekend play to three hours on most weekends and banned weekday play altogether. The Chinese government's draconian policies were meant to address the rising issue of gaming addiction amongst their youth. As a child who grew up playing Super Mario Brothers on Nintendo, where I would get awful blinking and frozen screens after playing for a couple of hours, I did not face serious risk of gaming addiction. But what makes gaming so intense that up to 10% of gamers struggle with gaming disorder?

To understand this, you have to understand basic tenets of game design. When you first start playing a video game, the designer's goal is to keep you playing the game. This leads to a start-where-you-are, learn-as-you-go model that becomes increasingly challenging as you become increasing proficient at the game's challenges. If video games started out at extremely high levels of difficulty, they would not be accessible and players would lose interest, quickly. If the games' difficulty leveled out over time and no longer created meaningful challenges, players would become bored and stop playing.

This productive struggle sweet spot, sometimes referred to as "flow," academically referred to as "The Zone of Proximal

DOI: 10.4324/9781003282464-16

Development," carries enormous implications for classroom instruction. Educators almost always desire a classroom where students joyfully engage in challenging critical thinking instruction. Making this a reality, however, is far more complicated. So often, the best-designed, well-intentioned critical thinking lessons fall flat on their faces for reasons that seem predictable after the fact.

Maybe you took for granted that students would know background knowledge and other schema needed to dig into content at a deeper level. Maybe you were caught off guard when students responded to your sudden use of open-ended questions with, "Can we just get a worksheet? I don't want to do all this!" Maybe the grandiose critical thinking task you expected would challenge your students were a walk in the park for your class. In any of these cases, we are missing the "flow." Fortunately, there is a concrete way to find that productive struggle sweet spot in our instruction: low floor, high ceiling.

The low floor, high ceiling construct allows educators to make critical thinking accessible to all students by allowing for a differentiated model of increased cognitive load. To be clear, critical thinking does not mean "harder, faster, more." And as I stated in Chapter 10 differentiation does not mean we are teaching to the middle students who are "too low" or "too slow" do not fall too far behind. The goal of the low floor, high ceiling construct is to engage and extend. This two-part goal requires educators 1) to create a concrete path for all students to engage in the most challenging level of critical thinking they can successfully access and 2) to create a concrete path for all students to extend their learning beyond their current capabilities.

This is different than how we typically educate children. Generally, we do not deliver lessons with an instructional framework aligning with "low floor, high ceiling." More often, we see lessons designed with more of a "low bar, high success rate in climbing over that low bar." For instance, I recall the joy I experienced when I uncovered buried treasure: pre-created worksheets and exams from my textbook that aligned with the chapter objectives! I was so relieved to see how much time I would now be able to save on designing all of these resources by myself. But I had a hard time figuring out why there were multiple versions of in-class worksheets and tests.

One set of classwork would be all multiple choice or simple computation problems with a couple of word problems. The other would be all complex, multi-step word problems. One test form would include straightforward questions that were multiple choice or simple computation problems with a word problem thrown in as a "bonus" question. The other test was full of challenging questions that required lots of application, critical thinking, and thorough written explanations of complex, multi-step word problems.

How could this be differentiation? The "easy" classwork and the "easy" test did not, in any way, reflect the level of depth and complexity required to master the assessed standard. The only thing these "differentiated" worksheets and test forms accomplished was to differentiate between students who would have access to appropriately challenging, grade-level instruction and those who would not. This "low bar, high success rate in climbing over that low bar" design model was a guaranteed way for me to sabotage my students' opportunity for academic success and making them feel good about it at the same time.

No educator needs a treasure trove of differentiated worksheets and test forms to fall into this trap. When you tell your "low" kids to answer those questions and your "high" kids to answer those other questions, I can almost guarantee the same inequity issue over access to grade-level content will be relevant. My intent is not to shame educators who engage in this process, willingly or unwillingly. The goal of highlighting this inequity is to share that this is a false choice: there is no reason educators have to pick between giving all students the "hard" version even though many will struggle unproductively or this fake version of differentiation. With low floor, high ceiling, educators can give all students the most challenging version of the classwork or test form while also giving them the differentiated skills, tools, and supports to tackle the challenge effectively.

The low floor, high ceiling process of 1) creating a concrete path for all students to engage in the most challenging level of

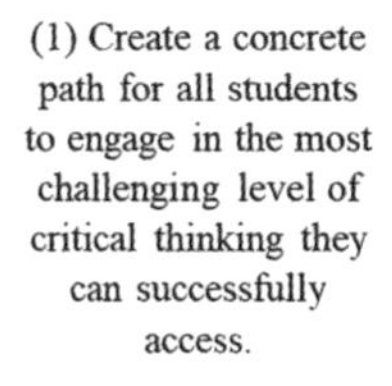

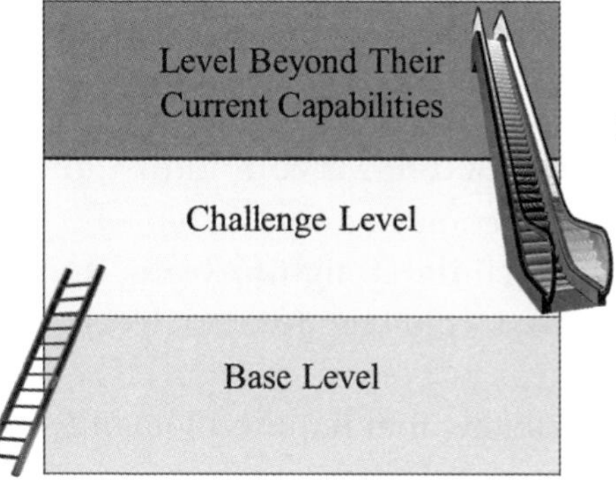

FIGURE 12.1
Two-Part Goal of the Low Floor, High Ceiling Construct.

content possible and 2) creating a concrete path for all students to extend their learning beyond their current capabilities is best explained through examples (Figure 12.1).

In math, suppose you are about to teach a lesson on percent change. According to pre-tests and your classroom data, you know that most of your students are struggling with the percent unit, generally. Ask ten teachers what they would do in this circumstance, and nine will tell you to reteach the percent unit enough for students to be successful in this current lesson. But if the lesson is about percent change, time spent reviewing percent is time not being spent reviewing percent change.

Part of creating the path for all students to change in the most challenging level of content possible is placing a strong bias against reteaching. Reteaching prerequisite concepts should only be done if it is absolutely necessary. This may sound intense, but it is not any more intense than the push a student who is two grade levels behind needs to make to end the year at or above grade level. As a nod to the benefits of gifted education as a tool to raise the bar for all students, discussed in Chapter 11, strategies to serve students in need of tremendous growth in a single year are similar to accelerated learners. The concept of curriculum compacting, typically used for academic acceleration, requires educators to be intentional about limiting grade-level standards to those that are absolutely needed to support acceleration. It is no great leap to understand, therefore, how a sixth grader reading at a fourth-grade level can benefit from the same acceleration techniques used to serve a fourth grader reading at a sixth-grade level.

Here, applying the strong bias against reteaching, understanding percent change does not truly require instruction on percentages.

The formula for calculating percent change looks like this:

$$\text{Percent Change} = \frac{\text{New Amount Original Amount}}{\text{Original Quantity}} \times 100$$

Even though percent change appears in almost every math curriculum's percent chapter, there is absolutely nothing about this formula that requires students to master percentages as a prerequisite. One of the most effective ways to create a concrete path for students to engage in the most challenging level of content possible is to stop obsessing about what they don't know and start leveraging what they do. For instance, students may not have mastered percentages. But, they probably know more about percent change than you are giving them credit for.

If you were to ask students to create a survival grocery list as an opening activity, listing no more than five items each, what would they put on that list? After the shenanigans that ensued at the start of the COVID-19 pandemic, we can probably presume that those five items would be toilet paper, toilet paper, toilet paper, toilet paper, and more toilet paper. That gives us a powerful clue about what students *do* know: price gouging. Supply and demand. An intuitive sense that as resources become more scarce, the price you are willing to pay for those resources increase dramatically.

Using this concept, you can connect students to the most challenging level of content through the example of the pharmaceutical company, Valeant. From 2010 to 2016, Valeant bought a lot of smaller pharmaceutical companies. When Valeant bought the other companies, they acquired new drugs. Valeant decided to raise the price of these medications. Students may not know what Glumetza is. Until they learn that diabetes patients rely on this extendedrelease medication so they only need to take one pill a day, and that without Glumetza, patients can experience heart disease, nerve damage, blindness, kidney failure, and amputated limbs. Then, they learn that within a six-year period, the price of Glumetza started at $350 and spiked to $5,148. At this point, this is no longer a percent change problem. This is a life and death problem. This is a fairness and justice problem. This is a problem students already have all the prerequisites needed to tackle.

Low floor, high ceiling also allows us to create a concrete path for all students to meaningfully extend and deepen their learning. Here, your students can serve as an aide for their congressional representative, helping her prepare for a hearing where Valeant will have to testify about their practices. "I don't do math" kids who despise the black and white nature of most math problems can enjoy the inherent funk of creating biased graphs. From the consumer advocate perspective, students can mess with the scales to create jaw-dropping visuals. of price gouging or par-for-the-course, steady increases over time. And I am certain the lawyers for the pharmaceutical company would use a very different scale to ensure their price spikes appear far more modest.

Like most things in education, successful implementation of a low floor, high ceiling framework is easier said than done. The next chapter will give you several practical strategies for managing this shift, followed by several additional chapters on classroom-specific instructional moves, frameworks, and curricular modification ideas to make Tangible Equity sustainable.

Part IV

Tangible Equity at the Classroom Level

13

Building the Low Floor, High Ceiling Ladder

Tangible Equity asks educators to take their existing content and rework it so allows for more and deeper opportunities for students to lead, innovate, and break things in such a way that accelerates the learning outcomes. Part of this work involves creating paths for all students to successfully access challenging critical thinking instruction and extend their learning. This chapter will break down the 9 + 1 checklist to help educators build the Low Floor, High Ceiling ladder (Figure 13.1):

Finding the Funk

It is one thing to say teachers should find opportunities to infuse funk, drama, controversy, and conflict into their instruction. But the "how" for this process is not necessarily something that comes natural for many educators.

To find the funk, think through the content you will be teaching in the next couple of weeks. And consider the following questions as you search for the most appropriate lesson to funk up (Figure 13.2):

DOI: 10.4324/9781003282464-18

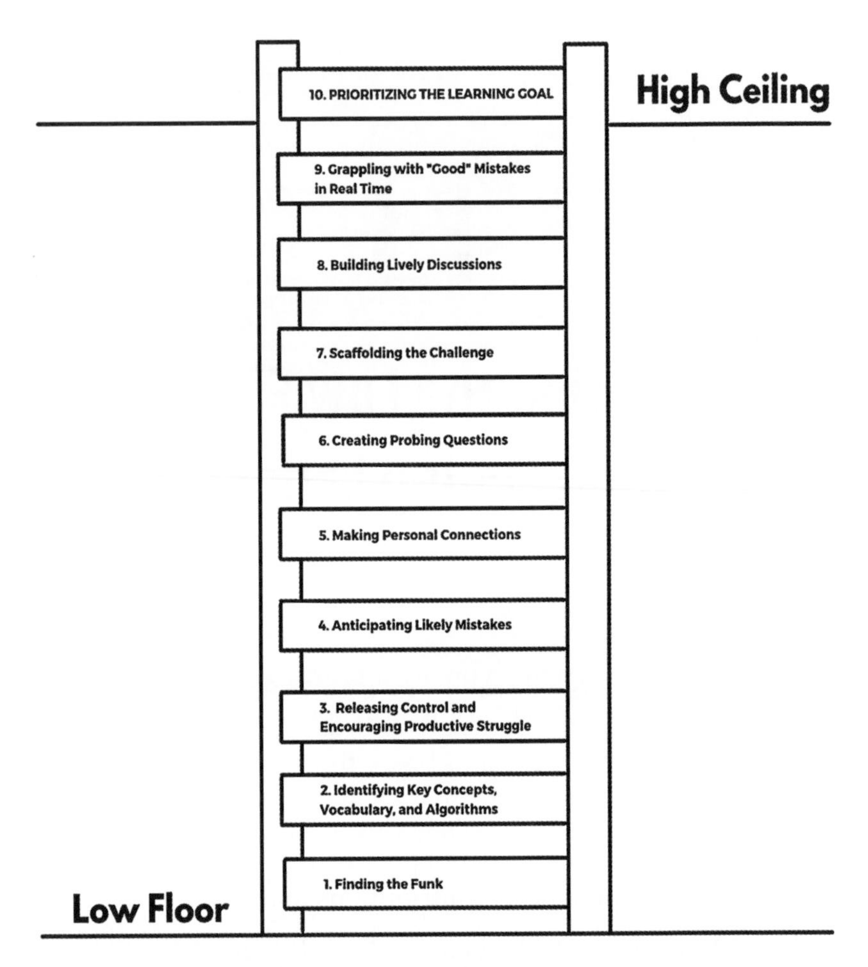

FIGURE 13.1
9 + 1 Critical Thinking Checklist for Building the Low Floor, High Ceiling Ladder.

There is one additional opportunity for funk that may not appear all that obvious: reviewing for tests. Jeopardy-style games or quiz-like apps are an easy, but low-level way to review previously covered material. But imagine if you had just finished an English and Language Arts unit on the parts of speech. Instead of doing a basic review along the lines of "identify this part of speech," students had to rank which parts of speech are the most important and why. Identify which part of speech, if eliminated,

Funky Element	Why is this Funky?
Is there a rule?	Rules are meant to be broken, proven wrong, extended to the point of absurdity, evaluated, and revised.
Are there interesting or weird characters, concepts, or events involved?	Characters or concepts that stick out are great fodder for mock trials, "what would you do in their shoes," or "what makes this so weird" deep-dives.
Is there something to compare, contrast, or rank?	Why do articles have titles like The 20 Best_____of All-Time? So readers can view the article, disagree vehemently, and help the article go viral through everyone else's desire to offer their input on this list.
Does the concept lend itself to multiple perspectives?	If "it depends" is the answer to a question, this question creates opportunities for students to shift their thinking based on seeing a situation from the perspective of others.
Is there an opportunity for a real-life call to action?	A lesson can lead to students writing to public officials, creating tangible solutions, and organizing for change, this builds their ability to model Tangible Equity by being the change.

FIGURE 13.2
Finding the Funk.

would have the most negative impact on making sense of the English language.

To model this, imagine you are a fourth-grade teacher planning out the next four days of instruction on Antarctica where students will have to:

1. identify where Antarctica is located
2. explain why there are not people in Antarctica
3. identify Antarctica's contributions to the world
4. identify and explain how the basic human needs of food, clothing, shelter, and transportation are met

Of these four, which standard is the most ripe for transforming with funk? It seems like identifying Antarctica on a map is very straightforward. Explaining why no-one really lives on a barren, frozen continent is probably also very straightforward. It comes down to identifying Antarctica's contributions to the world or explaining how Antarctica's residents meet their basic human needs of food, clothing, shelter, and transportation. There is a three part tie-breaker analysis when there is a close call like this: which standard (1) can best be taught in a way that also covers the other(s); (2) gives students a greater opportunity to use their own judgment to deepen the learning experience; and (3) provides for more natural extension activities.

Here, Antarctica's contributions to the world are probably something students, at best, would have to research. But once they research it, there is not a whole lot of obvious ways that students can use their own judgment to deepen their learning. Whenever contributions are at play, teachers can always find some funk by asking students to consider which contribution was most significant. The standard for exploring the basic human needs of food, clothing, shelter, and transportation, however, is far more interesting. Why? Because Antarctica is a weird place! It is the most ridiculous continent on Earth, in my opinion. If I want to get funky, thinking through this interesting problem from a personal level can be illuminating. Specifically, how can I, as a student, figure out how to successfully live in Antarctica.

Using this standard, you can design a lesson with an interesting challenge: Phoenix, Arizona is simply too hot (which is almost always a true statement). Your school just won a special grant from the United States government to move your school to Antarctica for a year. Every family will receive all expenses paid for this trip plus five times whatever monthly income they bring in. All you need to do is create a one-page plan that explains how you will ensure your school communities basic needs of food, clothing, shelter, and transportation will be met in Antarctica.

Finding the funk is not enough. Educators should also think about how to use what students already know to prepare for the funk and how to extend this funk beyond the classroom. Using this Antarctica example, I can start my lesson with a warm up/Do Now/bellringer activity that asks my students in Phoenix, Arizona, to give advice to a fourth grader in Alaska who is coming to visit Phoenix in July. My students may not know much about Antarctica. But they know about how to deal with the sweltering heat of Phoenix summers. They know that all the nonsense about "well, it's a dry heat" does not mean anything because 118 degrees is still 118 degrees. This activity is a scaffold that acts as a low floor, high ceiling ladder to access the critical thinking that lies ahead.

Extensions can be a bit more challenging. One way to think about extensions is to consider the "why" behind the lesson. Why are students learning about Antarctica to begin with? Yes, it is part of their standards. But what is the true value of students being able to understand how to overcome barriers to food, shelter, and transportation in Antarctica? Maybe the true value comes from understanding that no matter where you live on the planet, some people in your community also have barriers to food, shelter, and transportation. If your students could figure this out in Antarctica, nothing is stopping them from figuring out how to overcome similar barriers in their own communities. Finding the funk is not simply about problem-solving, it's about problem-finding. Incorporating this funk is key to the transformational education students need to not just play the game, but to slay the game.

Identifying Key Concepts, Vocabulary, and Algorithms

Identifying key concepts, vocabulary and algorithms is a straightforward, yet surprisingly overlooked aspect of designing lessons involving challenging critical thinking activities. This reminds me of a social studies teacher who felt like beating her head against the wall when she attempted to create a classroom simulation to teach students about the unbearable conditions of factories prior to the passage of workforce safety laws. She set up this amazing lesson where students were making teddy bears through an assembly process. The problem was, all students really cared about was making the coolest teddy bears, and the key concepts were lost on them.

Name all of the key concepts. Explicitly teach the academic vocabulary needed to access the content effectively. Explicitly teach the auxiliary vocabulary needed to access the *context* effectively. Provide clear algorithms, procedures, and step-by-step methods where applicable, and find as many opportunities as possible for students to create their own clear algorithms, procedures, and step-by-step methods.

Learning key concepts, vocabulary, and algorithms involves much more than just taking notes and regurgitating information.

Knowing what a concept means is meaningless if students cannot make meaning out of that concept. For instance, define mitochondria. If you learned the definition that most educators I work with across the country learned, you probably robotically recited "the powerhouse of the cell." But what does that mean? Why is the mitochondria important? Are you aware that not all cells have the mitochondria? Is a mitochondria-less cell still a cell without power? What if we discussed the scientific theory showing that fragments of the mitochondrial genome (which comes from mothers) in humans could be traced to a single woman ancestor living over 150,000 years ago? Or discussed that mitochondria dysfunction contributes to cancer, Alzheimer's disease, and Parkinson's disease?

When it comes to academic language, all students are learning a foreign language. Making meaning of content-specific vocabulary often allows for opportunities for students to make a personal connection. I was not sure how my students would respond to this type of thing, but students surprised me with their response to short story vocabulary challenges.

In a unit on solving multi-step equations, for example, a student who was always involved in some sort of drama cracked me up with her short story which went something like this: "I am so tired of all these variable females at this school, always coming in and switching it up. I want my friends to be constant so I don't have to keep guessing which version of them is going to show up today. You want to be constant? I will be your coefficient and just stick to your side. But there is no equation that will allow me to be friends with someone who wants to be some different every day. There is no solution for that!"

"I don't do math" students may hate fractions. But if they love playing music, that's a perfect opportunity for "math and": Fractions connect seamlessly with rhythmic patterns, time signatures, and the length of notes in musical pieces. Budding hip-hop artists might find graphs of trigonometric functions far more compelling when "math and" leads student rappers to understand beats per minute as the frequency and class DJs to recognize the period as a value that shifts based on slowing down or speeding up a beat loop.

Releasing Control and Encouraging Productive Struggle

Direct instruction still matters. The urge to engage students in deeper learning can sometimes get educators thinking that "stand and deliver" has no place in the classroom. This is not true. What makes teaching with a Tangible Equity focus look different is the rapid transfer of power from educator to student when it comes to doing the heavy lifting in learning. For instance, if I am a social studies teacher teaching my students the definition of "revolution," I will start by defining it as "a forcible overthrow of a government or social order in favor of a new system."

The transfer of power immediately follows when I ask students to tell me what a revolution is like. My students are not know-nothing, empty vessels. They have the ability to make connections, inferences, and do much more heavy lifting in their learning than we typically give them credit for. Students will likely know or infer that revolutions are often violent, political, and involve a lot of change. I can ask my students for examples of a revolution, where some of them may have either lived through revolutions or remember learning about The Revolutionary War or The Cuban Revolution. Releasing control and encouraging productive struggle is about getting students to think more, sooner.

This concept is especially important when teachers help students. In my workshops, I often ask teachers to help me out as a struggling reader who is having a hard time pronouncing the word "intersection." I keep getting stuck and have a hard time sounding out the word. When I ask for help, occasionally teachers just bail me out immediately and tell me the word is "intersection." Some educators explained to me that they do not believe in allowing students to get stuck on a word because they prefer students get the overall meaning of the sentence. I respond by saying that this is not an issue of belief: a student needed assistance on reading a specific word and the teacher did not allow that student to have any ownership or power to answer any part of the question.

More often, teachers respond to me by asking me to sound out the word. They ask me if there is any part of the word

I recognize. They guide me though, syllable by syllable, helping me push through. These probing questions are far more helpful for my learning because it helps me engage in greater levels of productive struggle. But there is still a big problem here: probing questions can be a gateway drug for help addiction.

Have you ever taught or known a young person who was literally addicted to help? This looks like a student receiving a worksheet and one second later saying, "Mr Seale, I need help!" This annoys me no end because I know that there is no chance that this student read the directions or even attempted to try before seeking a bailout. Students without any physical limitations who "need" help opening their milk carton at lunch every day. The most frustrating? When students are taking a test and come up to you during the test to say "Mr Seale can I get some help on this question?" This is a test! Why are you asking me to help you on a test?

I realized that students asking me for help on a test were not truly asking for me to answer the question for them. They wanted a "hint." More specifically, they wanted me to give them some helpful probing questions. Over-using probing questions can create a high level of teacher-dependency. It is no wonder, then, that students often struggle to complete complex word problems in math or science. Students become accustomed to their teachers asking them lots of guiding and probing questions for every problem they complete in the class. This ends up looking just like me using my GPS system to get to my destination. I get there, but I have no real clue of how to get there in the future because I never really had to think about it myself.

This is why I ask teachers to ask the same initial probing question every time: what question or questions should you be asking yourself right now? If I am struggling to read the word "intersection," and I ask you what this word is, your response should be "what question should you be asking yourself right now?" Because maybe I actually have some strategies my disposal. Maybe I can ask myself the same questions you are asking me, but I would never know that if you do not give me the opportunity to do so. If, in fact, I do not have any strategies at my disposal, this would just be a struggle, not a productive struggle. You would have to reteach me the strategies or start your probing question process. But if I want students who can persevere through the problem-solving process, students who are not just problem-solvers but problem-finders, and students who can lead, innovate, and break what needs to be broken, students need to be able to guide themselves through challenging situations.

Anticipating Likely Mistakes

An important part of teaching key concepts, vocabulary, and algorithms is to anticipate likely mistakes and to proactively plan for addressing these. If I am teaching students to convert words into algebraic expressions, I know that "four less than a number" requires me to define a variable for the number and subtract four from that number. The correct expression would therefore be "x–4." But I know, without question, that some students who look at this problem and automatically write this out as "4–x" because I have seen enough of this common error with "less than" algebraic expressions. I may even have some students write this out as an inequality, 4 < x because they confuse "less than" with "*is* less than."

In the culinary career and technical education baking course, I am sure teachers are not surprised when some students confuse baking powder for baking soda. You know how students will get confused when adding fractions with unlike denominators. You can predict that some students might confuse fact with opinion when the statement is "pizza is the best food ever" (because it is, even though adding pineapples to pizza is still a major controversy).

But don't stop at identifying WHAT students may do incorrectly. Make sure you think about WHY the mistake may happen so you can do a better job in your instruction to show them HOW to prevent that mistake. For instance, if a student tells you that 5 + 2 = 6, you should anticipate this to be a common mistake that occurs when students start their counting with an addend, which sounds like, "Okay, starting with five, I'm adding two, so five, six. The answer is six."

Making Personal Connections

Personalized learning has always felt like a redundant term to me because learning almost always involves some sort of personal connection. I recall the lightbulb moment when I realized how to put my shoes on the right feet. My mother used to always tell me to look at the shoes and make sure they match with my feet, and it never made any sense to me. Then one day, I really looked at the way my feet curved and the way the shoes curved and it finally clicked. Learning is all about the personal connections that come with those click moments.

When looking for opportunities to make personal connections in your low floor, high ceiling ladder, consider moments to ask students for their gut reaction to something or to make predictions or inferences. Recall that gut feelings are a way to leverage our students' identity, experiences, values, education in school, and education out of school. If there is a chance for you to press pause in your instruction and ask students to make predictions or inferences, this automatically builds a personal connection to the content.

Imagine, for instance, a lesson on the periodic table of elements in chemistry. Students can learn how the period table is organized like almost every chemistry student learns. But what if students were to work in groups where they received square cutouts of all 118 elements with the properties of each: number of protons, electrons, neutrons, atomic mass, year discovered etc. Might they have some ideas of how these elements should be sorted and organized? I can definitely see the value of an alphabetized periodic table because I remember the pain and suffering of trying to find the atomic number for Lead and forgetting that the abbreviation was Pb. If six groups worked on this, you would probably receive six different answers. And when you presented them with the actual periodic table of elements, they would probably look at it, nod their heads and say, "I guess that could work, too."

The personal connection here means so much more than designing questions that include their names and their interests. This personal connection is much more about The Learning

Relationships Triangle discussed in Chapter 9 (Figure 9.1), where you are finding opportunities to connect them to the content, to their scholarly community of classmates, and to their community beyond the classroom.

Scaffolding the Challenge

I created the thinkLaw curriculum because I knew how motivated students would be to unleash their critical thinking skills if we leveraged their inherent sense of justice and fairness. When I designed the first thinkLaw investigation and discovery lesson, I presumed students would easily be able to look beyond the obvious. But when I created a lesson based off a real-life scenario involving a tragic shooting, I realized that looking beyond the obvious was not that obvious.

The lesson was about a man who heard his doorbell ring and answered it. When he opened his door, he saw three people outside of his door and one who appeared to be holding a gun. So the man closed the door, grabbed a gun from underneath his bed, opened the door, saw a flash of some sort, and shot the person who appeared to be holding a gun.

I thought that in that moment, students would be able to seamlessly engage in the critical thinking challenge involved in determining what likely occurred in the next thirty minutes, what witnesses would be helpful in understanding what is going on, and what questions could help to clarify what occurred. But I realized that this was much more complex than I originally thought. Students were not used to this type of investigatory framework and had a hard time digging beyond the surface.

This real-life tragedy occurred on Halloween, where the three people were children dressed in costume. The man's son was killed in the Vietnam War, and the man was still traumatized from that death. When the man saw one of these boys dressed in military attire for a custom, fake gun and all, it triggered a panic in the man that turned to tragedy when one of the boys took a picture and the flash scared the man into thinking he was being attacked. But they would never have figured this out had I not scaffolded the thinking.

It is 8:30 am. You have ten dollars. At 11:30 am, you realize your ten dollars is missing. You did not spend it. What questions do you need to ask to figure out where your money went? This was the line of questioning I used to model the type of thinking students needed to successfully prepare for the investigation to come. Students suggested retracing steps or asking people about the money. But few asked questions like what day of the week was this or whether this was a ten-dollar bill, a five and five singles, or a roll of quarters. After practicing the process of thinking through non-obvious questions, asking non-obvious questions for the lesson itself was a lot more successful.

Before doing a complex lesson involving patterns, consider scaffolding the critical thinking with a simpler pattern. Before diving into a plan on moving your school to Antarctica, have students consider how they would prepare a friend from a different climate to live in their community. Whatever the challenging activity is going to be, ensure that you build some kind of low floor, high ceiling ladder to support some students who may need this to be successful.

Remember, this is not about supporting "low" students. The reality is, plenty of students who achieve at high levels in traditional classroom settings will struggle through more abstract critical thinking activities with no clear right or wrong answer. Also note that releasing control and encouraging productive struggle still applies. The frequency and extent of critical thinking scaffolding used in September and October should be more limited by March and April.

Building Lively Discussions

Few things are more frustrating than expecting a vigorous, lively discussion in class and ending up with lots of students with eyes like deer in a headlight. When "no talking" is the default rule in many classrooms, productive discussions do not occur without thoughtful planning.

As a teacher by day, law student by night, I would often look at the smirking professor who let a funky question fly like "a prosecutor withheld evidence and made several procedural errors in making a case against a serial killer who proudly confessed to committing his crimes, forcing the judge to release the serial killer. Does that make sense?" The professor smirked because she knew what was about to happen: students would immediately take off in a debate where some would talk about strict adherence to criminal procedure, some would talk about what this would mean to the victim's families, some would think about the safety concerns of releasing an admitted serial killer back to the street. And this would be an engaging, back and forth dialogue with lots of points matched with counterpoints. Why would the professor smirk? Because the professor was so confident that once she let that question out, she could be a fly on the wall, sit back, and watch students take this discussion to a whole other level.

This is not nearly as common in the K-12 classroom. Even when students are eager to discuss something, it typically looks like the teacher asking a question, followed by a student answering it, followed by the teacher responding to the student's answer. This ends up being a highly controlled environment that does not resemble the lively discussion we hoped for. On the other extreme, I have observed teachers who set up Socratic-style seminars where students would have more freedom to discuss amongst themselves. But the freedom was questionable given that one grading rubric I saw only gave students full participation credit if they spoke at least three times, responded to another student at least twice, and asked at least one question. Instead of deeply listening and authentically responding, students were merely waiting for their turn to speak. They care more about earning their points than they did about making, responding, and truly listening to points.

I know that many teachers love the look and feel of Socratic Circles, where the inner circle talks and the other circle listens and evaluates. But this is not an authentic discussion model. Socratic Circles do not exist in boardrooms, college lecture halls, or living rooms hosting book club meetings. And because I am somewhat militant when it comes to wasting time in the classroom, I do not see a lot of value coming out of the time lost in setting up and undoing the concentric circles required for this activity. I see even less value in a model where all students do not get ample time to practice the powerful skill set involved in learning how to listen to understand, speak to be understood, and disagree without being disagreeable.

To create more lively opportunities for discussion, consider setting up a classroom expectation where students do not have to raise their hand for you to call on them, but raise their hand to respond directly to other students. Instead of doing the extensive planning for a Socratic Circle, consider doing a much simpler fishbowl activity where one group models effective discussion for two minutes and the class gives them feedback on it. Then, split the class in half, conduct two fishbowls and have the split observers provide feedback. At that point, when you put the entire class into groups, best practices would be much clearer to students.

Grappling with "Good" Mistakes in Real-Time

No matter how well you prepare by anticipating likely mistakes, there will always be some students who surprise you with the mistakes they make. Prepare for these by using these moments to maximize productive struggle for that student and for the rest of your class. Questions like, "what makes you say that?" "based on what evidence?" and "explain how you got that answer" can be extremely revealing.

I grew up in Brooklyn, New York in the very Caribbean neighborhoods of East Flatbush and Canarsie. One time my daughter, Rose, asked me if my best friend Kali's mom had 20 brothers and sisters. I said no. She then asked me if his dad did. I also said no, but I had to ask her why she is putting me through this strange line of questioning. It turned out that she was very confused by the Caribbean custom of calling most adults who were close family friends "Auntie" or "Uncle" even if there was no blood relation. She was paying attention, making mental notes, and trying to make sense out of something that did not make sense. But if I did not take the time to interrogate her thinking by grappling with this "mistake" in real-time, I would have missed out on a chance for me to understand her confusion and for her to understand a piece of her cultural heritage she would rarely come across in Phoenix where the Caribbean population is far less.

Grappling with mistakes in the moment involves patience, empathy, and understanding. Every time you model this process when a student makes a surprising mistake, you are also modeling beneficial social emotional learning skills other students can see and internalize as a way to improve conflict resolution skills.

Prioritizing the Learning Goal

The entire point of the Tangible Equity model is to give students the tools they need to succeed in and beyond the classroom. Succeeding in the classroom mandates a focus on learning outcomes. But for some reason, educators often have a tendency to get loosy-goosey around formative assessment and learning goals when critical thinking instruction is involved.

The truth is, learning goals need to be even clearer when deeper learning is involved. In traditional lesson planning, it is usually a lot simpler to teach key concepts, give students practice on those concepts, check their understanding as you go, reteaching as necessary and do an exit ticket at the end of the lesson to see how they ultimately did at mastering the day's objective. If the lesson is about how people in Antarctica overcome barriers of food, shelter, and transportation to live there, it requires a bit more focus and intention to ensure students really get it.

Prioritizing the learning goal involves a three-step questioning flow: 1) What do they need to know; 2) do they know what I'm doing right now; and 3) did they learn it. The first step is all about ensuring students have the perquisite information to successfully complete the critical thinking activity. Note that this is not just about content, but also about context (Figure 13.3).

I thought I was being very clever when I incorporated a real-life case about a car accident that involved a plaintiff suing a defendant based on the claim that the defendant ran through a red light at an intersection. A witness observed how far the

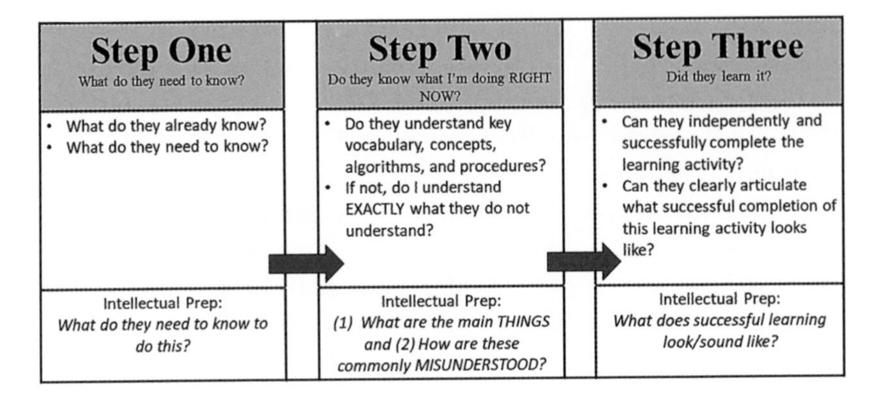

FIGURE 13.3
Three-Step Questioning Flow.

defendant was away from the stop light when the light hit yellow. This was a great opportunity for students to practice unit conversions and several mathematical formulas. The problem was, so many of my students who did not drive or have drivers in their families did not understand what was going on at this intersection. Fewer knew what a plaintiff or a defendant was. And surprisingly, several students thought that a yellow light meant that it was time to go very, very fast. Considering the driving patterns I've seen living in New York City, Washington, DC, Las Vegas and Phoenix, maybe that is not actually all that surprising.

The second step is the same type of formative assessment process you do in the earliest stages of teacher prep programs. If you know what all the key concepts, vocabulary, algorithms, and procedures are, you must continuously assess that students demonstrate their understanding accordingly. One of the best ways to prepare for this is to plan, in advance, for how the key things are commonly misunderstood. This gives you a chance to fine tune your look-fors as students engage in independent work. It also is a chance to spark higher-level discussions on mistake analysis by purposefully teaching with mistakes in mind. This may look like analyzing two paragraphs that both have poor organization and asking which "wrong" is more "right" (i.e. which should get a higher score on the grading rubric).

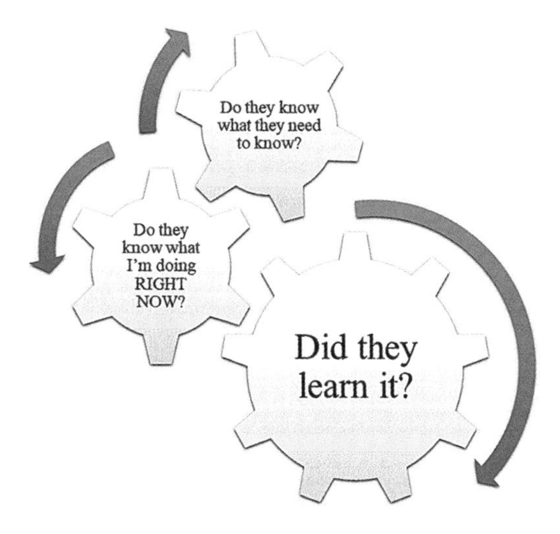

FIGURE 13.4
Three Cog Wheels.

Last, and definitely not least, before you can access whether students have met the learning goal, you must determine what successful learning should look and sound like. Ideally, students themselves should be able to articulate the success criteria for the lesson. It may seem extreme, but when educators are new to this process, it could be helpful for teachers and students alike when teachers prepare sample student work in advance to get a clear picture of what exemplary, mediocre, and subpar work would look like.

This is not always a linear process. Sometimes, for instance, you may realize students do not understand what you are doing right now and you have to backtrack to step one to determine what precise prerequisites may be missing, jumping later to step three to make sure they actually learned during that review. Thinking about this as a questioning flow that can go in multiple directions is a helpful visual for remaining flexible as you prioritize the learning outcome (Figure 13.4).

Putting it All Together

There is no magic bullet for designing the type of instruction that helps educators equip students to lead, innovate, and break what

Critical Thinking Technique	How will I use this technique in my lesson?
Finding the Funk Where can I add in conflict, a real-world problem, "What if..?" scenario, ranking, or other opportunities for funk?	
Identifying Key Concepts, Vocabulary, and Algorithms What do students need to know to successfully complete this lesson? What do they already know?	
Releasing Control and Encouraging Productive Struggle How will I make sure students are doing most of the heavy lifting?	
Anticipating Likely Mistakes Do I know the most common mistakes and misconceptions with this material? Am I prepared to address them?	
Make Personal Connections How am I connecting the lesson with students' real-life experiences, interests, or current events?	
Creating Probing Questions Do I have a list of probing questions prepared throughout the lesson that will lead to a rigorous discussion?	
Scaffolding the Challenge Did I make time to link the previous learning and review relevant vocabulary?	
Building Lively Discussions Am I prepared to keep the conversation constructive, civil, and on topic? Where could it go wrong? How can I avoid that problem?	
Grappling with "Good" Mistakes in Real Time Am I prepared to respond to students' good mistakes during the lesson? How will I remember to press pause and take advantage of these learning opportunities?	
Prioritizing the Learning Goal How will I know ALL students meet the learning goals of the lesson?	

FIGURE 13.5
9 + 1 Critical Thinking Checklist for Building the Low Floor, High Ceiling Ladder.

needs to be broken as an integrated part of accelerating learning outcomes. The 9 + 1 checklist for building the low floor, high ceiling ladder is therefore not the be-all, end-all for this process. It merely gives educators a helpful guide for increasing the success probability of this type of instruction prior to delivering a lesson (Figure 13.5).

14

Discussing Controversy without Becoming the Controversy

When I was first approached to do an equity workshop, I initially objected because I did not believe that thinkLaw's explicit focus on powerful, but practical critical thinking strategies for educators and families were what they were looking for. I was correct, somewhat.

Teachers and education leaders reached out to me because they were eager to play a more active role in addressing our nation's racial injustices. Some of them wanted training in how to talk more about racial injustice in school, even as early as kindergarten. The reality is, my children learned about racial injustice first-hand when they were in pre-school. That education comes fairly quickly when a little girl tells your daughter "you weren't invited to my birthday party because brown people aren't allowed at my house" and when that same little girl tells both of my children, "that's why no-one likes brown people." I get why teachers and education leaders wanted more support on this. I wish my kids' former school leaders sought out this kind of support instead of suggesting that this little girl's Black uncle, my daughter, and this little girl worked together on a project to learn more about why you shouldn't be racist to Black people.

DOI: 10.4324/9781003282464-19

Still, I would be hesitant to say that it is extremely important that all teachers know how to speak to students, especially young students, about racial injustice. Here's the way I look at it: the events of January 6, 2021 when rioters violently stormed the Capitol Building in Washington, DC were something that was probably on every educator's mind and on many students' minds on January 7, 2021. As much as I may believe that it would be a great thing if all educators were prepared to have a meaningful discussion the next day to help them process their emotions or make sense of such a shocking event, I am certainly not alone in being thankful that not all educators attempted to do so.

It would be extremely hard for educators who in many cases have not had the personal time to understand or process a single event on a single day to turn around and effectively deliver any sort of meaningful instruction about it. And these are the adults in the building. It would not be a stretch of the imagination to presume that students likely would have a harder time understanding or processing this event on a single day.

This is why I when I get requests from educators and education leaders about how to meaningfully talk about racial injustice in school, I typically have the same reply: don't. If a single, shameful day of modern history can have such a shocking impact on the psyche of adults and children, educating students as young as five years old on hundreds of years of racial injustice is not something I would feel comfortable accomplishing, even in multiple professional development sessions.

This has nothing to do with avoiding politics in the classroom because I am a firm believer that education is inherently political. My Political Science 101 definition of politics is instructive in exploring these questions: Politics is "who gets what, where, when, and how." It is impossible to separate politics from education when education is the largest direct expenditure of every state's government. "All politics is local" takes on a much deeper meaning when school funding beyond the state government is determined by local property tax revenue or when the always-contentious issue of school zoning boundaries is up for debate. From COVID-19 reopening plans to school transportation options for students (or the lack thereof), there is no shortage of politics in education, and that's before we even start talking about what actually happens in the classroom.

This has everything to do with my belief that educators should only bring up potentially controversial issues in their classes when they have established the psychological safety, classroom climate and culture, and civil discourse needed to do so. The question, then, is how do educators discuss controversy without becoming the controversy?

To be clear, I am not suggesting that teachers shy away from tackling the important issues of the day. It would be completely hypocritical for me to suggest avoidance when Tangible Equity requires students to get the tools they need to both succeed in our current system and dismantle and rebuild it to be more just and equitable. But it would be a wildly unrealistic expectation that today, students are working on worksheets printed from your standard district curriculum, but tomorrow, you expect to successfully have a classroom debate about transgender bathrooms.

Now, more than ever, any sort of classroom debate has a high potential of going off the rails, even when it is not about a hot-button issue. When students even hear the word "debate," most students do not think about this as a thoughtful exchange of ideas with well-stated points, counterpoints, and well-supported evidence. They think of a brawl! It seems unthinkable now, but I recall my high school English teachers suggesting we watch the Sunday news shows to boost our SAT vocabulary knowledge. Now, the only reason I would watch these news shows is to learn how to own my opponents and not answer any questions.

The key to understanding the balance between discussing controversy without becoming the controversy is to focus on the civil discourse trifecta. First, we ensure students know how to listen to understand. Second, we ensure students know how to speak to be understood. And third, we ensure students know how to disagree without being disagreeable.

Getting to this level means students must learn to walk before they learn how to run. You would not teach calculus to someone who does not know solid multiplication facts, so learning how to engage in civil discourse around touchy topics is also something that requires scaffolding. How do we do this? With two strategies that shut down the controversy before it starts: starting early and tying to standards.

Starting early means that we do not wait until middle or high school for students to engage in civil discourse. Instead, we prioritize the development of the underlying skills needed to create a foundation for civil discourse. With education conversations increasingly focused on social-emotional learning, it can be easy for teachers to feel like "okay kids, its time for our SEL block" instead of integrating SEL seamlessly into existing instructional practices and classroom cultural norms. But starting early allows educators to teach in a way that recognizes that you can feed multiple birds with the same worm. And if you thought I was going to say we could kill multiple birds with the same stone, then you are the reason why we can't have nice things.

Instructionally, starting early could look like asking students to use a more critical lens towards nursery rhymes, fairy tales, and other children's story to consider multiple perspectives. Consider this brutal example of exploitative child labor:

> **Little Boy Blue**
>
> Little Boy Blue, come blow your horn,
> The sheep's in the meadow, the cow's in the corn.
> Where is that boy who looks after the sheep?
> He's under a haystack, fast asleep.
> Will you wake him? Oh no, not I,
> For if I do, he'll surely cry.

I get that at some point in human history, subjecting little boys to hard labor was totally acceptable. But imagine kindergarten students trying to figure out why this young shepherd is slacking on the job when you press pause after "Where is that boy who looks after the sheep?" Now, they have to make inferences about where they think this boy might be. Maybe he is in school? Maybe he is out playing with his friends? You can ask who is looking for him? His parents? His boss? Are his parents his bosses? Then we realize he is sleeping under a haystack. Sleeping anywhere around hay does not seem all that comfortable. Sleeping underneath hay seems even worse. Is he hiding? Not too sure, but if waking him up guarantees that "he'll surely cry," maybe there is a reason he is hiding.

This may sound humorous, but it is actually a powerful way to build empathy. When young children get ample opportunities to place themselves in the shoes of others and analyze stories from perspectives other than the narrator's, it creates a habit of empathy. This is one of those "soft" skills that are exceptionally hard to teach and seems to get harder the older students are.

Starting early also means releasing power to help students solve their own interpersonal conflicts. This is not to say that teachers or parents should look the other way at serious reports of bullying, threats, or actual physical harm to children. As time-consuming and frustrating as false or exaggerated reports of bullying may be, no school administrator would ever want to be responsible for overlooking a serious incident. At the same time, however, we have little hope as a society if children grow up depending exclusively on the adults in their lives to solve their problems with other children.

My daughter attended a play-based pre-school when we lived in Las Vegas that blew my mind as a parent. I arrived a little earlier than usual one day and Rose was playing with a toy. A little boy came to her and said "can I play with that please." And I, like any "helpful" parent would do, said "Rose, please share." And her teacher quickly contradicted me and said, "Rose, no. What do you say?" And Rose responded with, "I am playing with this right now. You can play with this toy when I am done."

My initial reaction was outrage. What madness are these people teaching my child? Don't you know we are trying to live in a society here, people? But then I realized that saying no to things you do not really want to do is a life lesson in balance that most adults struggle with. Then I realized that if children at three and four years old can politely decline, accept disappointment, and agree to disagree, they are getting set up a future of civil discourse that is leaps and bounds beyond the nonsense we adults do with each other today.

Tying "controversial" teaching to standards is equally important. It is worth noting, again, that education has never been apolitical, in or outside of the classroom. This goes beyond hot-button classroom issues like whether sex education is taught in school or whether schools use anti-racist curricular resources like The 1619 Project.[1] In 2019, for instance, the New York Times studied the same company's textbooks used widely for American history in Texas and California to show that the different state's versions told two vastly different stories. The inherently political nature of education is undeniable.

Before discussing how discussing controversy without becoming the controversy is a part of almost every state's educational standards across grade levels and subject areas, consider the following question: Which of the following is too political to be displayed in a public school teacher's classroom?

- We hold these truths to be self-evident, that all men are created equal.
- One nation, under God, with liberty and justice for all.
- O say does that star-spangled banner yet wave o'er the land of the free and the home of the brave?
- I have a dream that my four children will one day live in a nation where they will not be judged by the color of their skin, but by the content of their character.

It is hard to imagine angry parents screaming at a school board meeting because a teacher had the words "We hold these truths to be self-evident that all men are created equal" hanging in his classroom. But is it really apolitical to deify a document calling for overthrowing the government in the name of equality for a select group of white property owners? Similarly, reciting "One nation, under God, with liberty and justice for all" would never lead to discipline. But is it apolitical to promise to be loyal to your country under the condition that it offers liberty and justice for all? And even though this next phrase reads as an explicit directive to question the extent of equity in our country, a poster asking "O say does that star-spangled banner wave o'er the land of the free and the home of the brave?" would probably not be labeled as anti-American propaganda.

I also cannot imagine a teacher facing discipline for hanging up the full text of Dr King's "I Have a Dream" speech in her classroom. It might be different, however, if instead of blowing up the "content of their character" quote on the top of the bulletin board, a teacher decided to prominently display the excerpt of this famous speech that said, "the Negro still is not free." The same goes for Dr King's not-so-universally-loved line from this speech, "America has given the Negro people a bad check, a check which has come back marked 'insufficient funds.'"[2]

There is almost no doubt that this would lead to pushback. Phrases like these might be hard to hear. They may rub listeners the wrong way. Students, parents, and even some educators themselves may become defensive when they hear lines like this. But these statements, while tough to hear, are factually accurate. And when it comes to policing political speech, school systems certainly cannot justifiably set a standard that would allow educators to cherry-pick the lines of documents and then decide to penalize people for highlighting excerpts deemed "too political" when they accurately call into question our country's aspirations toward equity.

State standards provide such a powerful justification for diving into this work. In Texas, for instance, English I standards require students to "write persuasive texts to influence the attitudes or actions of a specific audience on specific issues."[3] At a time when some are concerned about schools teaching indoctrination to children, the fundamental of the first course in high school English is literally designed to teach students how to indoctrinate! For first graders, the standards ask students to "work collaboratively with others by following agreed-upon rules for discussion, including listening to others, speaking when recognized, and making appropriate contributions." These standards mandate that educators start early to help educators listen to understand, speak to be understood, and disagree without being disagreeable.

Alabama requires sixth graders to "critique major social and cultural changes in the United States since World War II."[4] Not to study or analyze major social and cultural changes, but to talk smack about these changes. Third-grade students in Alabama are similarly mandated to not learn what to think, but how to think, as they "distinguish their own point of view from that of the narrator or those of the characters." North Carolina expects environmental science students to "explain how human activities impact the biosphere" and requires third graders to editorialize as they "write opinion pieces on topics or texts."[5]

Texas, Alabama, and North Carolina do not exactly have a reputation as states that want to indoctrinate their students into becoming climate change activists and bleeding-heart liberals. The reality is, that this is and has never been about indoctrination or controversy. This is about learning. Critical thinking. Engaging students in deeper learning opportunities. And creating a new normal where we no longer purposely shy away from politics, religion, and money to be polite, limiting our society's ability to have any sort of meaningful conversations about politics, religion, and money.

Notes

1 *The New York Times*. 2019. "The 1619 Project." August 14, 2019, sec. Magazine. https://www.nytimes.com/interactive/2019/08/14/magazine/1619-america-slavery.html?mtrref=www.bing.com&gwh=BABAECD58EC23B6BEAE692083F051809&gwt
2 King, Jr, Martin Luther. 2017. "'I Have a Dream.'" The Martin Luther King, Jr, Research and Education Institute. May 8, 2017. https://kinginstitute.stanford.edu/encyclopedia/i-have-dream
3 Texas Education Agency. 2019. "Texas Essential Knowledge and Skills." October 10, 2019. https://tea.texas.gov/academics/curriculum-standards/teks/texas-essential-knowledge-and-skills
4 Alabama Learning Exchange. n.d. "Courses of Study: Social Studies (Grade 6)." October 6, 2021. https://alex.state.al.us/standardAll.php?grade=6&subject=SS2010&summary=2
5 NC DPI. n.d. "Standard Course of Study." https://www.dpi.nc.gov/districts-schools/classroom-resources/academic-standards/standard-course-study

15

Mandating Joy

This is not hard work. This is heart work. The challenge in front of us as educators, as family members, as a community can feel overwhelming and daunting. Achieving true equity means we will reduce the predictive power demographics has on outcomes to zero. This does not mean that outcomes will be the same across the board. It will just mean that demographics would no longer be such a strong predictor in determining those outcomes. This would mean that stories like mine involving a first-generation immigrant who grew up on free and reduced lunch, and had an incarcerated father and still received an amazing education and flourished professionally would no longer be an exception to the rule. We are in the business of changing this rule altogether so that all children will have a legit shot at being exceptional.

But this is not easy work. It is hard enough to say we need to bring students to academic levels of success so they can be college and career ready. But with the Tangible Equity Equation we are pushing for with this book, we are asking educators to focus on academic success and educational justice. To focus on giving students the tools they need to navigate the inequitable system we have today and giving them the critical thinking and leadership skills they need to make our system more just and more fair. This work rejects the tunnel vision of playing the game

DOI: 10.4324/9781003282464-20

in favor of a dual vision of playing the game while learning how to slay the game simultaneously.

None of this is easy today. None of this is going to be easy tomorrow. And even if you find yourself gaining all sorts of momentum in your classrooms, schools, and homes with implementing the strategies in this book, that momentum will not be easy to sustain. If you are a teacher or school administrator who made it to the end of this book, I would take the "over" odds on whether you received less or more than three new major mandates from your school system from the time you started this book to now. Mandates are inevitable. Mandates can be extremely distracting, no matter how much you have committed to your equity priority and no matter how much you have worked on transforming instruction to make Tangible Equity real at the classroom level.

So, what do you do when you cannot figure out how to focus on Tangible Equity while also focusing on whatever the next mandates coming down the pipeline are asking of you? You mandate joy. Joy is a revolutionary act in education today. Mandating joy in classrooms is an extreme act of defiance. For so many students in our nation, laughing and learning at the same time is a privilege. Even before the concerns of extreme learning loss from the COVID-19 pandemic, many of our students who are most in need of the transformational education this book calls for were least likely to experience joy in their learning. It is completely unacceptable to force those students to have even less joy than before by forcing them to do massive amounts of drill and kill intervention and remediation. When we decide to take away electives and specials so students can sit in front of a laptop with headphones on to play catch-up, this is the opposite of mandating joy.

When I talk about joy in learning, I go back to this goofy dance the cool kids on the math team and I would do when we all got a problem right. I think about teaching the kind of classroom where at least once a week, I got the knock on the door with one of my annoyed neighbors saying, "Mr Seale I don't know what you are doing in here but you all need to tone it down." It never occurred to me that there was any other way for

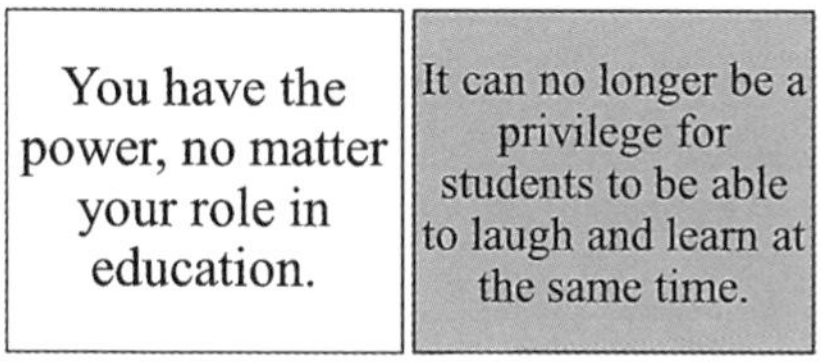

You have the power, no matter your role in education.	It can no longer be a privilege for students to be able to laugh and learn at the same time.

FIGURE 15.1
You Can Mandate Joy Daily.

students to learn. Talking is just thinking out loud, and students need to be thinkers.

Joyful classrooms lead to joyful teachers. This is not just about being liked or a generic idea of building relationships. This is about doing what "liked" teachers do by creating classroom environments full of challenge, helpful feedback, and intrinsic motivation to push through meaningful challenges. This is about prioritizing a learning relationship where students joyfully relate to content, joyfully connect with their classroom peers as they learn, and joyfully connect their learning to be both the problem-finders and the problem-solvers our communities need (Figure 15.1).

Tangible Equity is a destination that will take lots of work on lots of levels to ever become a reality. But you can mandate joy daily. You have the power, so use that power no matter what your role is in education to mandate joy. Because it can no longer be a privilege for students to be able to laugh and learn at the same time.